The Doctor Can't See You Now

Reflections of a Retiring GP

Dr David John Maddams

The Doctor Can't See You Now

First published in 2019 by

Panoma Press Ltd
48 St Vincent Drive, St Albans, Herts, AL1 5SJ, UK
info@panomapress.com
www.panomapress.com

Book layout by Neil Coe.

978-1-784529-04-8

The right of Dr David John Maddams to be identified as the author of this work has been asserted in accordance with sections 77 and 78 of the Copyright, Designs and Patents Act 1988.

A CIP catalogue record for this book is available from the British Library.

This book is available online and in bookstores.

DEDICATION

To all my friends at Dolphin House Surgery
and NHS staff everywhere – you are truly amazing!

TESTIMONIALS

"Very powerful, honest and raw with humour thrown in. It blew me away."

Angela Spencer, child health author

"Very funny, sad and honest all at the same time."

Dr Clare Gerada MBE, past chair of Royal College of GPs

ACKNOWLEDGEMENTS

With thanks to my stepdad (my 'dad' for 56 years) who believed in me enough to encourage me to be the first of the family to go to medical school.

Love to my mum, who died at a ripe old age just before publication and would be saying as she often did, "I don't know where he came from," which is a bit disconcerting!

Much love to my doctor wife Jane for putting up with me and doing her medical training in geographical reverse to me so we met in the middle. Luton was so romantic!

Love and admiration to my medical kids Jess and Alex who are two of the kindest people I know and will make amazing doctors.

Thanks to Dr Peter Martin GP of Laindon, Essex who showed me as a medical student that GPs were awesome and to his colleague Dr Ranvier Bass for honing my GP skills as a trainee GP.

But mostly, a huge thank you to the people of Ware, Hertfordshire for letting me be their GP and confidant for over 31 years. A remarkable privilege which I will always treasure.

PREFACE

Age 59 and with 35 years of experience of being a doctor, I decided to write down my thoughts and experiences as I started to complete what I envisaged would be my final year as a GP during one of the NHS's most difficult times in its 70-year existence. Things were so bad that NHS staff were leaving in droves and the service was close to breaking point. Many excellent GPs younger than me had already left.

Would I manage to hold on for another year or would I go the way of others before me? As I reminisced about my former years as a doctor all kinds of memories and thoughts came to the surface. Why did things need to change for change's sake anyway as many developments in the year were having a negative impact on family doctors? Were we seeing the end of general practitioners as we have known them? Then there was the problem of was I ready to retire? What would become of me and my patients? Clearly my final year would be far from straightforward and what would be the outcome in the end?

CONTENTS

CHAPTER 1

THE BEGINNING OF THE END?

My 59th birthday, January 29th 2018, was meant to be the day I would suddenly feel better. After all, the NHS was in free fall and I could easily retire a year from that date aged 60, having been a family doctor for over 30 years and part of the NHS pension fund since 1982. I envisaged ticking off the days one by one saying that's the last time I will ever have to do this on this particular day. It was bound to feel awesome. I would be grinning from ear to ear all day. With all this experience behind me I was a truly fulfilled and complete doctor with just 365 days to go and counting.

Unfortunately, things in life are never as you expect. For a start I was slow off the mark getting my holiday request in and was pipped at the post by two colleagues also wanting that day off. Then I found that if I was to work I would have to be on call as the duty doctor. More misery! Then having had his operation for cardiac surgery delayed, my dad was called with a revised operation date: January 29th!

Oh how I loved the NHS and the winter of 2017/18 when everyone except our government came to the conclusion that the NHS was broken, or if not broken had a severe case of dysentery. Everything that winter seemed to be going down the pan.

Then there was the thought: did I actually want to retire after all? What would I do instead? Since 24 years of age being a doctor had taken up a huge chunk of my life. I could see this year was not going to be as straightforward as I had originally planned. It now felt complicated. I felt ill at ease. The grin had definitely gone.

Hopefully as the year progressed I would come up with an answer. I would feel better about all this, or would I?

Everything in medicine and general practice had suddenly become very complicated that January. With doctors and nurses finding the pressure too great they were actually leaving the NHS in huge numbers. In fact, over three months recently, more than 200 GPs had quit early. A far cry from when I started out and there had been 200 applicants for my GP trainee post. However, the thing that galvanised doctors more than anything during the cruel flu-stricken winter of 2017/18 was the case of Dr Bawa-Garba. Everyone working in medicine was suddenly in shock.

The story goes like this. A junior hospital doctor, returning from her maternity leave and therefore presumably not fully back up to speed, was found guilty of manslaughter when a poor unfortunate boy with Down's syndrome in her care died of septicaemia. Mistakes were made. However, it turns out that hospital IT systems were down so results were not getting back to the medical team in a timely fashion. Dr Bawa-Garba had been reported as covering up to five colleagues due to staff shortages. The most senior doctor supporting her was not at the hospital. She then made the fatal error of not resuscitating the boy thinking he was another patient.

Without doubt, the whole truth about the case needed to be heard and lessons needed to be learnt. Certainly those who failed him needed to be punished appropriately. But what happened next has sent the profession into apoplexy. The General Medical Council overturned the lay tribunal decision to suspend her and instead had her struck off. That's it, game over. Not being a doctor anymore. Damned by one case. How many had she saved up until then?

So as of this month every doctor or nurse is left wondering what if I make a mistake? People make mistakes in their jobs don't they? What is bad enough to be found guilty of manslaughter and to lose one's medical career where making life and death decisions is a regular daily occurrence? And what now the health service is under serious pressure with lack of resources and lack of staff? Who's to blame now?

The debate has just begun and will take some sorting. Even the present health secretary Jeremy Hunt has raised concerns as he can see a situation where mistakes will be buried and not acted on. How did we get to this point? It seems hard to see any easy way out. But I'm now on my way out, in about a year. Hopefully, there will be no major incidents before then. Perhaps I am leaving just in the nick of time. I start to feel a bit more relaxed about leaving, but only just.

Then of course there is a chance that there might be a case that pops up in the future for which I have been paying handsomely for insurance cover for years. About £14,000 per year for my doctor wife and me. GPs are independent contractors so we are not covered by the government like our hospital colleagues. Seeing how the increasingly large premiums are putting off new GPs and encouraging others to leave early, the government has suggested this might change. Premiums have dropped for some in anticipation but there is great uncertainty (again) about what will ultimately happen. We keep being told there is no extra money in the NHS so how can this be sorted? I then realise that having produced two kids that are part of our future junior doctors, I might sigh with relief, but their anxieties are only just beginning. How I hated this bleak and unforgiving January and the state of medicine just now.

It is very stressful working 12-hour days as a GP, without having to support a sick relative as an inpatient in a London hospital recovering from major cardiac surgery. Being in his 80s it was never going to be straightforward for my dad, but we hung on to the fact that he was very fit for his age and his grandfather had been 102 when he died! I suppose we do that as human beings and try to latch on to any glimmer of hope. In fact, he was in for the whole month, initially doing well but the operation was delayed so 'he could be stabilised' and his fluid balance addressed. Then, when we thought all was well postoperatively, he decided to work through every known complication as any relative from a medical family is apt to do it seems. Medical family members never behave well when ill or in labour. Take my word for it.

My wife and I would rush from our surgeries to catch trains or tubes depending on what line was blocked that day. I came to have nothing but admiration, or was it pity, for my London commuting patients. However, being hospitalised in Chelsea does at least mean a ready supply of nice little eateries, albeit quite expensive ones, especially when you do a whole month of hospital visiting. We did manage to enjoy a belated birthday dinner, used some vouchers for a brasserie in Sloane Square we had forgotten we had been given, and even managed an overnight stay in a boutique hotel just a 10-minute walk away from the hospital. But then I remembered we were meant to be having a week in the Madeiran sun. Suddenly cold and frosty Chelsea and Kensington weren't half as inviting.

I had also managed to master my Oyster card for the first

time. A bit like the first time I walked into IKEA, I found repetition eventually meant I got the idea of it. However, for the last few years I won't actually touch a real oyster ever since that is, my wife was so ill, she is convinced she nearly died after eating one measly oyster. In fact, several people have. After her experience I found out that up to 50% of oysters can be contaminated with Norovirus (the winter vomiting virus), yet people still say they love to eat them; that is except a famous chef and a restauranteur friend of ours who don't offer them anymore, for fear of manslaughter I suppose. This chef holds the record for one of the largest food poisoning outbreaks of all time by the Norovirus in oysters.

All credit to our secondary care colleagues working in our overstretched hospitals this winter. However, I always like the opportunity to observe and take in the differences between primary and secondary care when I can.

During the whole time my dad was on his ward, his name label above his bed never indicated his consultant or lead nurse. Every day I went in it was with positive expectation. No luck. A blank space only. To this day I still don't know who had ultimate responsibility for him and nor does he, and yet wasn't there an initiative declaring that every patient had a right to a plaque over the bed and a named consultant? I don't know about you but if the government has to have a fanfare-blowing initiative to get this done on every ward then the NHS is in serious trouble. Why do hospitals need a directive in order to do this? Isn't it just something they used to do? As it was, it was really quite hard to get information at all and I prefer not to use the 'I'm a doctor you know' ploy if possible.

It's actually quite hard to know who to approach on a ward even as a medic. I have found before you cannot assume the ward sister knows what's going on with all patients these days. I found sometimes I would pick someone who said ask so and so when they come in; they never did come in. Sometimes we struck oil and had a very informative doctor or nurse we could quiz who appeared unexpectedly at the end of the bed.

The trouble is that as a medic your relative speaks a different language from you and has a different concept of biology from you too. They often relate what the doctor has said and it makes no sense at all. They seem to have all kinds of connections between organs going on that no one else has or should have, all sorts of inappropriate procedures planned and potentially lethal cocktails of drugs being offered when the sole source of information may be an elderly man bordering on postoperative delirium! You know they are talking garbage but you can't always get the true story. I pity the non-medical relatives, they haven't a chance.

I hope in primary care we are better at saying who we are and what's going on. As most patients have chosen, often repeatedly, to come and see you as their doctor, it's easier I suppose. I do however think communication is still a major factor in our hospitals today.

In general practice hours and hours are spent as a trainee GP videoing and practising consultations and communication skills including giving information to patients. The easiest way to instil fear in a trainee GP is to talk about the CSA – the Clinical Skills Assessment. An expensive exam for debt-ridden postgraduates, held at the Royal College of GPs in Euston in London, where anyone who wants to be a GP has to act out a dozen or so clinical scenarios with specially trained actors and an examiner looking on over three hours.

If you do not demonstrate people skills and fail, then all that hard work over years at medical school and in foundation years in hospital will be in vain. You get up to four goes if your educators agree and manage to secure funding to stay longer in your trainee post. It causes the most angst in my trainee GPs I work with, and as it so happens my daughter took it this month so I know from first-hand the worry it causes.

Now, I have only been in hospital once and it's very scary. Not only is it odd being 'on the other side' but generally the fact you are a medic makes no difference. In a way it's a good thing to feel that vulnerability but then you are dying – literally it feels at times – to be acknowledged for who you are and to tell people that you have some inside knowledge and are a colleague. During my stay I had the bizarre experience of my legs being used as a nurse's writing table for the theatre nurse who approached the trolley I happened to be on. At first she dropped a huge pile of notes on my legs. Oh she's gone and broken my legs, I thought.

Initially I was shocked, confused and felt vulnerable and put in my place; was she someone who had a grievance against doctors perhaps? Would she be instrumental in my post-operative care? Then I started to chuckle as the absurdity of the situation came into my mind. This produced a frosty glare as if I was mad. Not something to do too well in a medical establishment; no telling what mental health section order you might end up with. Eventually, the notes were removed, I confirmed my legs weren't broken and still worked. My own records however were still on my legs and she scribbled something in them and then left. I've never seen her since. She never uttered a single word during the whole ludicrous process. I assume she passed the nursing version of the CSA at the fourth attempt!

Having survived the operation I convalesced on the private wing; I told my wife it had been suggested I did this otherwise my own patients that happened to be on the NHS ward would stare at me and get twitchy. Doctors aren't meant to be ill you see, especially if it's your own GP. It unnerves people. Actually the truth is I liked the sound of the chicken tagliatelle with a glass of Chianti on the menu, but I didn't tell her. Four days later I was back at work and did a night shift. I would love to tell any patients into their fourth week off after the same procedure to man up, but then I hate confrontation these days.

Luckily, I haven't needed to go into hospital since. I did need a follow-up appointment for a check cystoscopy however. Basically, a camera rammed through the penis to the bladder. Of course as a GP, I know a lot of the consultants. So when you have a procedure you generally know the person. Now that's fine, but when told here comes a small scratch and a little sedative to help the procedure go smoothly I was expecting to be a bit sleepy. In fact I was out cold and had no idea it was all over until I awoke in a pool of dribble and wondering if I said anything rude or revealing whilst under the influence to a fellow colleague. Much better had it been a stranger. Too late to worry, but I had to pinch myself in case I had gone back to private care as I was offered an amazing NHS frothy cappuccino with a selection of the poshest biscuits Jeremy Hunt could afford. Worth the scope I thought.

A nursing sister on the unit reminded me to stay put and buzz if I needed the loo. What seemed like five seconds later, another sister popped her head round. "How are you?" she said. "Amazing," I said looking at the cappuccino. "Pop your clothes on then." No sooner had I my hands on my trousers to pull them up I noticed the untouched cappuccino had gone. Did I catch a glimpse of a theatre nurse running away giggling, cup in hand, or was it the anaesthetic? Oh, I need the loo, shall I buzz? Oh no, it's down that corridor, turn right then left then right again, off you go.

I so wish secondary care would stand back and look at themselves sometimes. How can I go from a vulnerable post-sedated patient one second and then a caffeine depleted fully independent has-been patient the next? I am always saying to my trainees to put themselves in the patient's shoes. They think it odd at first but they eventually get the idea. 'Hello my name is' is catching on, perhaps 'what's it like in your shoes' could be next?

So here I am. One month into my last year as a GP. Confused, tired even more so than usual and wondering what am I to do in the year ahead. I am grateful my dad finally did OK and the medics did enough to get him home, and I myself was not a patient in hospital during the complex wintry start to 2018.

CHAPTER 2

MARCH/APRIL

TEA, BISCUITS AND RAW FISH

The end of February and the beginning of March saw an extremely cold snowy spell and thoughts turned to cruelty. Not just the cruel weather. There's talk of people dying on our streets due to the increasing number of homeless individuals sleeping rough in extreme temperatures. Patients are expiring waiting too long for ambulances. People are being treated or dying in hospital corridors.

The unbelievable thing is that although there is the usual outcry over such things, it seems there is no real desire to put it right quickly. Are the people in the right positions to affect change no longer interested or touched by this? I find it depressing to live in our country if this is to become the new norm. Surely having the confidence of an ambulance arriving in a timely manner when seriously ill and an emergency hospital bed available when you need it has to be a right we can all expect in our wealthy well-off country.

Part of my role as a GP and GP educator is to read trainee e-portfolios. These electronic records of learning are filled in on a six-monthly basis with patient case reflections called logs. At the moment that's about 300 of them per six-monthly assessment. I read this week a case log by one of my trainee GPs of an upset patient and it hit a raw nerve with me. A lady suffering a second miscarriage was told that there was no capacity for a scan that day as she had ceased bleeding so was not in immediate danger.

However, a repeat miscarriage was suspected so she should return the next day for a scan to confirm this.

The junior doctor reflected on this in his log and the cruel nature of this policy. He seemed to have stepped into the patient's shoes. Having been on the end of this policy previously I could feel the emotion. I could put myself in the patient's shoes as they had been mine once. How can this be right even if resources are tight? She needed to know for sure, have her procedure and get home to start the grieving and healing processes. Things like this count a lot and yet I bet practically every ultrasound unit in the country will have this same rule. It should not have to be this way.

Equally cruel is the way couples are treated when infertile. Yes, the NHS cannot pay for everything, but you see this cruelty at work when finance meetings deciding on what gets funding lump infertility services in the same finance meeting as paying for tattoo removal. The suggestion is that the people on that committee haven't tried on many patients' shoes recently. This actually happened in my own patch and totally underestimates the impact of infertility on a couple.

If we are going to regain our compassionate nature as a nation perhaps we need to look to the top for guidance and to take a lead from those who govern, but our politicians seem very tarnished and not listening enough these days. There are plenty of passionate people in politics but we could also do with a dose of compassion just now.

Today my daughter passed her CSA exam with flying colours and I had an interesting silver embossed card in the post from the Royal College of GPs president congratulating me on 30 years' membership and asking for feedback. I was so chuffed with my ever so little and unexpected card. Funny how the small things can make all the difference. My son came home from medical school with Norovirus as he was out of starchy foods. He denies eating oysters!

The news this week focused on the demise of education, and teachers' workloads especially leading to a recruitment crisis. The government is going to sort it. The same government that is who are pushing for extended opening hours for GP surgeries. When I started out we worked as a practice 24 hours a day, 365 days a year, all done between the five of us of which my wife and I were two fifths, and a bit of cooperation across weekends with a neighbouring practice. It could be really tough if you were up all night but generally you had a full or half day off afterwards. It was a really cheap system as you would get about £11 per patient visit if up between 11pm and 7am the next morning.

There were extra payments if the callout was to a patient not on your list, if seeing a whole family, and for other services including, would you believe, the arrest of a dental haemorrhage! Quite what a GP with two days of dentistry teaching at medical school was meant to do to stop said haemorrhage, nobody seemed to know, but to have such a challenge and enhance one's salary seemed very exciting in the mundane world of the late 1980s. Oh, and if you were really clever you could gain another fee by asking the patient, if a lady, about her contraceptive intentions as you forced the cotton wadding into her dental socket. You might even make £50.

All these regulations and more were contained in the so-called Red Book. It was called that because it was a red-covered book and nothing to do with Chinese politics. It's funny now to think that I received my regulation red book in person when I started as a GP. I was invited, along with the senior partner in the practice at the time who would later emigrate before things turned nasty, to meet and have the chat from the chief executive of what was called the Family Practitioner Committee. Tea and biscuits, a quick hello, here's your red book and have a nice career. These days you would be hard pushed to know who is who, and frankly in a world where there are NHS managers out there actually allowed to run expensive conferences entitled 'Do We Need GPs At All?', I can't see a tea and biscuit session happening anytime soon. I really should look out my red book. It could be worth something in a few years, on *Antiques Roadshow* perhaps.

Of course, being part of the old order it eventually succumbed to the Carr-Hill formula. An ingenious idea by the eponymous professor, from which the formula takes its name, in order to do away with all the form filling and book reading. Basically, every practice had its income calculated by this unique formula. Sounds great doesn't it, except things and circumstances change. Imagine bouncing along thinking everything was great with your formula estimate when somebody comes along and builds a Butlin's or a Center Parcs next to your practice. Suddenly your estimated temporary resident payment looks very inadequate.

Also payments like educational allowances and sabbatical payments were 'hidden' in the total. Imagine saying to your cash-strapped practice, "Hey guys, I'm off to deepest Bolivia for 12 months, hope you don't mind holding the fort, and by the way just withdrawing the £10,000 you owe me." It just won't happen, which is a shame as sabbaticals can be a lifesaver.

Back to extended hours. Basically, all governments are paranoid. They must be regularly losing sleep over public servants not working hard enough and pulling a fast one.

Politicians also have a serious overdose of 'we know best'. As a consequence, in all the years I have been a GP, apart from perhaps the first three years or so, there has been a drive to fill up the time doctors have on their hands with as much as possible. It was a shame because as we did our nights and weekends with a minimum of moans and almost for free, we also retained continuity of care, and by knowing our patients, kept a fair number of folk out of A&E departments.

The consequence of all of this has been tired GPs giving up night work within practices and transferring over to out of hours services. Back in 1988, I didn't feel guilty spending an hour or so on a summer afternoon away with my new baby daughter as I would be working an average 10-hour day and possibly 24 hours if on call. It seemed everyone was a winner as being a salaried doctor doing the nights and weekends was part of it, the only extra payment being after 11 at night as mentioned earlier.

At first the Family Practitioner Committee disappeared. I guess their crime was using all the NHS tea and biscuits. Then the community health screening paediatricians went. Just get the GPs to do it instead. Then the diabetic patients started to become the responsibility of GPs and leave outpatient clinics en masse at a time that we were starting to see an explosion in diabetic numbers. Notice here no extra GPs to allow for all of this and more. At present we have over 400 diabetics on our list, so if they are well as opposed to unwell and seen as suggested every six months, that is 800 appointments gone in one swipe. Imagine that. Then add on those who are unwell or poorly controlled and you are well over the 800 number. No wonder it's hard to see the GP these days. Isn't it a miracle you are actually seen at all and all credit to those who regularly try to run their systems as efficiently as possible to maximise access.

And so we are back to extended access, and why oh why now when the profession is saying we can take no more does the government insist on this? I would love to be available to my patients for more hours in the day, but even now most of us work 12-hour days due to the paperwork after the patients have all gone home by 6.30pm. So even extending to 8pm and part or all of weekends is going to be a problem. No time now to get the sunbed out in the middle of the day with your newborn bouncing on your knee. No chance seeing more of your favourite GP. They will be spread more thinly instead or perhaps they will have emigrated.

If there's one thing that upsets me these days apart from the politics of the NHS, it's homeopath bashing for all kinds of reasons. Perhaps I'm sensitive or deluded or both but it has seriously got out of hand. I see that it has hit the headlines again and even doctors are contributing to the vitriol against colleagues. I became a GP homeopath in the 1990s after completing a course in acupuncture beforehand. I became interested when my wife's uncle who used the stuff gave me a remedy which abolished some chronic symptoms I had practically overnight.

Now perhaps I was in admiration of this guy and hence the placebo effect. He was certainly a larger than life character with a booming Northumbrian voice, who had done well with a string of optician shops, a garden centre and various other investments. We loved him for his fun-loving character, originality and especially his old gold Rolls Royce. On one trip to stay with us he had driven it to pick up our Chinese takeaway, an image we will never forget, especially the looks he attracted.

However, I'm not so sure it's all placebo. I have seen similar miraculous recoveries myself when using homeopathy, only ever at the patient's request and when all other conventional therapies were exhausted, as well as awful skin eruption side effects following a predictive pattern when a patient overreacts to a remedy, and not a hint of placebo at all. Children respond particularly well, well below the age of knowing. Still there is a drive to strike off doctors like me or even burn us at the stake perhaps and all because it's implausible, which it is.

But what if it does work? Wouldn't we be missing a trick? An ultra-cheap nanomolecular treatment reaching the parts other medications cannot reach. The attackers say anything more dilute than the Pacific Ocean producing a chemical response is bonkers. However, these people fail to say and often don't know that enhancing the Brownian motion of particles, which homeopaths call succussion, is of prime importance when making remedies. I remember a British Medical Journal headline announcing homeopathy is rubbish. In fact, a trial using homeopathy to treat asthma showed that after three weeks homeopathy was statistically no better than placebo in reducing symptoms. The authors did conclude a few unusual things were possibly happening towards the end of the trial period. However, rather than saying homeopathy does not seem to improve asthma when given for three weeks, they went for the all or nothing headline. Homeopathy is proven to be a big pile of doggy do. Pretty scandalous for a reputable journal.

It's been downhill for homeopathy since. I prefer to keep an open mind. Same as I keep an open mind on the billions spent on finding the Higgs boson particle; the fact that Einstein's theory of relativity probably has a small kink in it; quantum physics has an entanglement theory; the Universe may be elongated in shape; and that there is in all probability some kind of God. It's interesting and useful as a family doctor to have an open mind when dealing with patients who come in all kinds of shapes, sizes and types, telling you the most amazing things that they get up to. I wouldn't want to lose that. Not for all the particles in the Universe.

March ended with a nice little break for my wife's 59th birthday over Easter in Stockholm. Our youngest has suddenly fallen in love with everything Scandinavian and made the suggestion; I think also the realisation that Mum and Dad bank was in a much more robust state for a trip to Sweden and the cost of living there. Actually we had a fantastic time and the weather, despite the cold, was awesome. Huge bright blue skies and near Mediterranean warmth if you were clever enough to get out of the wind and have the full glare of the sun. After the winter we had had my priority was vitamin D maximisation over protection from skin cancer. It's nice we still allow choice.

Going to Sweden allowed me to use the only bit of useful information I picked up on a trip to Finnish Lapland when the kids were small. That is you never need be cold. Layer up sufficiently and you can cope with most weathers and actually enjoy it. Unfortunately, most Brits tend to have a coat for all seasons that does for a rainy day in spring and doubles for a protective layer against a snowy day in winter, and it's never enough so we don't see any pleasure in the winter experience. I suppose the Scandinavians have had to adapt. One of the partners in the practice is half Norwegian and at the height of winter still comes to work in only a shirt. I dare say once we hit minus 25 the various layers would appear. Either that or he has a severe form of peripheral neuropathy and has lost all feeling. Nobody has asked him.

The other lesson from Sweden was that things are not always as they seem or you expect. I imagined it would be so clean we could eat our meatballs off the pavement. In fact, Stockholm was a bit scruffy post-winter as our taxi driver complained and explained. You see, everywhere around was a mass of grit. Clearly salting would not work at such low temperatures so they scatter tonnes of grit on the roads and walkways. Unfortunately, as the taxi driver explained, they have a massive sweep up in very early summer; apparently a recognisable spring doesn't always happen, but before then the grit is mixed with scraps of litter and thousands upon thousands of cigarette butts. The strange thing is I can't remember anyone actually smoking in the street. Perhaps the taxi drivers empty out their ashtrays in the street and blame everyone else.

The other thing for a capital city that struck me was you never hear an emergency vehicle siren. Either they have no police, a ban on sirens or very little crime. During a month when London's stabbing statistics became a national disgrace it seemed nice to think there are still major cities on our planet where people can walk without too much fear. The only thing that I was worried about was Diphyllobothrium Latum or the Danish Flatworm to be precise, or was it Finnish? Apparently a cause of anaemia as the worm sucks blood from the host's duodenum (upper intestines). It can be a consequence of eating raw fish which seems very much a national pastime in Sweden.

Now I adore fish but I have never seen the attraction of eating raw animal anything, and as this rather useless bit of information from medical school just won't leave my ever shrinking brain it keeps popping up and adding to my anxiety. Unfortunately, it has never raised its head in a pub quiz to date so continues to be a rather worthless fact.

Funnily enough another fishy tale stays lodged in my cerebral cortex and that is Erisipelothrix Rhusiopathiae. I seem good with fish. This time bacteria that infested the hands of fish workers. Well imagine my glee on a medical school attachment in the early 1980s in Grimsby when in walks a fish worker with dermatitis on his hands. The consultant in charge was livid as I don't think many medical students had made the diagnosis before and I kind of stole his thunder. I learned early on as a medical student that you were rarely congratulated on ward rounds whether you were correct or not.

My medical student kids say little has changed at times although there does seem a slight drop in consultant educationalists with psychopathic tendencies. They were all the rage in the 1980s. Quite literally. Perhaps that's why a lot of doctors walk around with a worried expression. Something my non-medical friends often comment on! Perhaps I should also enter a pub quiz in North Lincolnshire.

So Sweden, albeit a brief trip, was a huge success once I learned to choose cooked fish from the menu. I never saw a flatworm and didn't develop a rash on my hands so I guess I got off lightly. I still think memory is a strange thing. I struggle with names more and more these days but I remember these strange facts from medical school days. All very interesting but I bet they could shrink the theoretical bit of the medical school curriculum if they tried a bit harder.

Refreshed after my first break in five months it suddenly dawns on me that if I want to I can retire in under 10 months and I'm not fazed anymore.

Early April and apparently we are to get some new medical schools. It has finally registered with Her Majesty's government that there are not enough doctors. Maybe the health minister's cortex is becoming shrunken like mine, but talk about the obvious. Anyway, better late than never.

So where are they going to be? Well word has it places like Chelmsford, Canterbury, Lincoln and Sunderland. Now don't get me wrong, I have been to all these places and have nothing against them, but thinking how long it takes for a medical school to gain a reputation is this the right way to produce more doctors quickly and will people apply to such areas? Time will tell I suppose.

Someone out there with the right A-levels might like five years experiencing the North Sea coast or deepest Essex and its county town. I am also a bit bitter as I know my home county of Hertfordshire (to the north of London) lost out on a new medical school some years back to Norwich. As my county seems bursting at the seams with people but not hospitals, and patients have to traipse into London for some of their specialist care, filling up an overstretched transport system, I am disappointed to miss out again.

Hopefully, the government will also realise that GPs cannot go on absorbing more and more new housing estate residents and more and more new nursing home residents without some kind of expansion process. It amazes me that there is no good system in place to guarantee an adequate primary care service is in place to deal with this. The slow absorption of new patients, as we used to do when towns expanded by a dozen houses at a time, is no longer fit for purpose. In my own area we are yet to have our second large nursing home open in a year and have heard that our neighbouring practice wants to close their patient list as they cannot recruit replacement doctors. We are just holding on but May is likely to get very interesting. Maybe the practice will fold before I do.

Despite the gloom, we manage another trip away at the end of April and into May. My holidays this year will be like London buses. You wait for ages and then two come along. At least I can afford decent holidays and try and recharge once in a while. I am starting to wonder how this will pan out once I am relying on just a pension. Best not to think just yet. So it's off to our beloved Greece just as back home the temperature was due to drop to 8 degrees and have a month's rainfall in a day. It will be a chance to eat an extremely healthy Mediterranean diet, soak up some sun, but not too much to keep my dermatology friends happy, and take in the wonderful scenery of blue skies and turquoise waters. Definitely a wellbeing trip. In fact, looking at the diet you wonder why all Greeks do not live to 100. Perhaps it's the fact that a lot still smoke compared to other Europeans and live with the constant worry of if and when they will get their next pay packet.

I do love the M diet. Somehow when on holiday and the sun is out it's so easy to eat salad swimming in olive oil with a little grilled meat, fish or low fat cheese. Fruit too becomes all the more appetising. We leave and head back home with all sorts of good intentions but sadly the sun goes in, the temperature drops and it's back to traditional British grub. I always thought it a pity that one of the famous TV chefs hasn't come up with a sort of 'Briterranean' diet where UK meets the southern Mediterranean diet that would be easier to cook and eat in all weathers in the UK. A kind of roast beef dinner and Yorkshire pudding made with olive oil! Maybe not but you get the idea.

In reality, as a nation we need to get an idea pretty soon. The change that needs to take place to stop the monumental rise of obesity and type 2 diabetes needs to be ground-breaking, wide ranging and quick. Already there are 4.6 million people in the UK with the prospect of being joined by another 12.3 million at risk of developing diabetes.

I am at present the diabetes lead in my practice and the number of drugs, many of them expensive, needed to control the illness make me tremble with fear for the future. Far better to get to people before they develop it. The cost of diabetes in the UK is now 10% of the whole health budget and being spent at £1.5m an hour. So we are staring disaster in the face.

So the sugar tax might be a start but we are going to have to be a lot smarter than that. Everyone needs to get on board and the government is going to have to sell the healthy eating message over and over again and make some dramatic changes. Some will say it's a deprivation of a person's freedom of choice, but they don't see the money I see being spent on trying to deal with it.

I also think we are missing a trick with our elderly. It seems no one has thought of doing small one-sized meals with added nutrients for our older people, many of whom do not relish the thought of a standard meals on wheels menu. Yes, you can order meals to be delivered and frozen. Yes, not all meals on wheels are unappetising, but then some elderly people like going shopping or being taken shopping, and who, if I'm honest, can plan meals so much in advance when appetites and tastes can change from day to day? So I think the supermarkets would do well to launch a 'Silver Service' range with our older folk in mind. Meals for their tastes, at the right portion size and with the added nutrients required to keep you well in old age. I am convinced a better nourished older population would reap huge benefits for our NHS.

I am reminded of an elderly man I saw in a nursing home once. I was convinced he had scurvy. A lack of vitamin C. The same as I once thought a patient who purposely restricted their diet had developed beriberi, a lack of vitamin B1 also known as thiamine. Unfortunately, the chances of seeing such cases being taught at medical school on nutritional disease and being able to screen for such illnesses is practically zero. In fact, a recent publication this month suggests medical students in the UK get either none at all or just 10-24 hours of nutritional teaching over five to six years. Sounds like this too needs to be part of our national nutritional plan.

Anyway, back to scurvy. Interestingly, the home, which is rather a good one, was ticking all the right boxes for the Care Quality Commission inspectors. Freshly replenished fruit bowls were in all the lounges as additional food items to the daily menus. Unfortunately, no one had twigged that this slightly odd bedridden man, who was bed bound more due to his social phobia and personality than a physical disease, had no intention of ever venturing out to any fruit bowl. Besides, many older people would need help to peel and safely consume any such fruits. I often wonder if his poor skin, poor skin healing, bleeding and joint problems were more a case from Captain Cook's or Christopher Columbus's diaries than mine, but then there is no way of checking other than giving vitamin C.

There are no easy tests for GPs to check for many vitamin deficiencies other than vitamin B12, vitamin D and folic acid. Also no one has ever seen or considered these diseases in this day and age that we now live. But surely there must be cases. I doubt if any specialists exist out there that could advise a GP either. So as you can see nutritional teaching and a national nutritional plan is desperately needed. Food for thought. As for me I'm off for another fix of olive oil before we need to check out of our hotel.

CHAPTER 3

MAY/JUNE

COMING OF AGE
AND WAISTCOATS

There's been a lot of talk about the NHS being 70 years old this year and I suddenly realise that I have worked for it for half its existence and it feels awesome. Thirty-five years in this great institution. Isn't it funny how it never dawns on you when you start out that one day you will have clocked up enough time to be a 50% part of its history. In fact, I started a little sooner, which I was reminded of when I checked my pension data recently when preparing to consider my retirement date.

What had happened was I was called upon to act as the houseman on the ward as a senior medical student when the proper houseman went sick. Actually, it happened twice. Can you imagine the outcry if this was to happen nowadays? It was an amazing experience and put me in a much better position when I finally took up my first junior doctor post. I'm sure I was a better house doctor as a result and I cannot remember any patients being harmed in the process.

The first time, and this launched me on the NHS pension scheme, was during a student elective in Hastings. My best man was the hospital pharmacist and I fancied a cheap holiday on the south coast. As much as I loved my university in Sheffield there were some summers where I honestly believe the sun did not appear and so seven weeks by the seaside on Britain's sunniest coast seemed a good bet. No sooner had I arrived, one of the leading acute geriatricians of the time asked, or perhaps I was told, that I would have to do a two-week locum or else the department would not be able to function.

The prospect of a wage for two weeks made my mind up and so there I was in charge of receiving all the acutely unwell over-70-year-olds in Hastings. It would have been even scarier, as my registrar could often be called away to a neighbouring hospital, had it not been for the amazing nurses. To my great relief, as each patient came on to the ward, the sister in charge would have all the correct blood bottles at the ready along with X-ray request forms and appropriate drugs drawn up depending on the working diagnosis. All this would be followed by a cup of tea and a biscuit.

In other words, her experience was such she could have done the job standing on her head, but it was me that had to officially do it. It left me with a huge respect for the nurses and it worked both ways, which felt good. I also had loads of respect for the SENs on the ward. The nurses who had worked their way up from the bottom with huge amounts of practical common sense and empathy for patients as opposed to SRNs who generally did the more complicated stuff and studied nursing at nursing school. Of course these days nurses take a degree course and I am not convinced that this is right for all nurses or patients. I do hope to see various routes into nursing being available as options again, it seemed to work well.

The second time I was pressganged into an early introduction into being a junior doctor was when finishing off my senior surgical placement at Rotherham District Hospital. This time straight into an on call day with all the surgical team deep in the operating theatres below. So imagine my horror when my first patient was wheeled on to the ward with an acute abdomen. On feeling his tummy I could feel a large pulsatile object and it was no ordinary object. It was his aorta having a leak. Crickey! Could I, and the patient for that matter, be that unlucky at this stage to be faced with such a life-threatening event? So there I was, half an hour into the post, having to ring my ever so scary boss with his brazen Yorkshire accent and tell him to drop everything and return to the ward. Would I regret doing this, had I felt a giant poo and the pulsations at my fingertips were all mine?

Happily no. There was an absolute hush as the consultant made his own careful examination. Then he looked at me and took a big breath as I held mine. "Well done lad. Absolutely right. Getting him ready for theatre." I had survived my first hour as a junior surgeon. After that things got better and after much nagging from the surgical registrar, a nice Italian from Milan, I plucked up courage to ask to be considered for the job when my time came. I would go back for the mandatory six-month attachment the follow year. Oh, and the patient survived too.

I added a few pounds to my NHS pension but wouldn't know it until 35 years later. Little did I know it then, but on returning to the ward the following year I would be on call and the receiving junior surgeon on the day of one of the biggest and most brutal battles between striking miners and the South Yorkshire police to be seen in the early 1980s – 'The Battle of Orgreave'. Being a house surgeon was certainly a good way to have to learn to have one's wits about you very quickly. I'll come back to Orgreave later.

This month the news broke about the not so nice goings on at a geriatric ward in Portsmouth. Unexpected deaths seem to have happened all over the place and a doctor, a lady GP who was in charge, could be implicated in the unnecessary deaths. This story interested and scared me all at the same time for various reasons. The main one being that our practice looks after a 108-bedded elderly care unit with all manner of elderly care problems to navigate through in a very short time. About three to four hours a day to be precise and clearly it's not enough most of the time.

Within this facility that replaced a very old geriatric hospital and former workhouse in my home town there is also a 20-bedded unit of intermediate care patients. This is the new buzz word for what most folk would know as convalescence or rehabilitation. In short, elderly people come out of hospital after major illness or fractures and a wonderful team of nurses, physiotherapists and occupational therapists, which I have the pleasure to support with my medical knowledge, get them up and about and home with various forms of support called packages of care. Such a success has it been that we receive very complex patients that the hospitals cannot progress any further or who need palliative care. Often we receive patients with very advanced dementia.

All this is very challenging and here's the thing. Several years ago we were told that our cottage hospitals had to close as they could not support patients adequately enough. Everyone deserved the best that modern medicine could give. Not a money-saving exercise then. When I started out, our local hospital with its two old-fashioned medical wards served very well for an elderly person with, say, a chest infection and they didn't seem to get stuck in there either. Perhaps they did better knowing they were close to home and having close attention by nurses and physiotherapists with a manageable workload.

Now wind the clock forward and overstretched hospital wards with complex elderly patients semi-sorted are discharging patients to intermediate care with nowhere near the staff and facilities of my mourned cottage hospital. I have learned in my career that there is little logic in thinking when governments or NHS managers decide they want to do something. What is said one decade can be totally reversed the next, all for the 'good' of patients. Still I'm proud of what we achieve in our not so little unit.

Thinking back to medication and the elderly has reminded me that it's a bit of a minefield. Our policy has always been to reduce medication, particularly sedatives, to a minimum. Lots of elderly people come out of hospital on shedloads of tablets. I have had 100-year-olds discharged on a statin (cholesterol-lowering drug) for the first time despite no real evidence of effectiveness in the time they have left on Earth. I often have dementia patients on at least three major sedatives. We often will reduce these with incredible results including so-called palliative patients becoming no longer palliative. Hence my interest in the Portsmouth story.

However, this policy is not foolproof. Families still complain and scream at times as we are seen to 'go against the hospital'. As a consequence we have had to announce that this is our policy and please let us know if this causes problems. I know in an ideal world you would let every relative know about every single thing you are doing or plan to do to their loved ones, but there aren't enough hours in the day so you just hope you are doing what most folk would see as a well-intentioned plan of action. Of course we aren't all the same folk and are primed and affected by all kinds of things said, read about and broadcast. Portsmouth is likely to have done us no favours.

In the summer of 2018 England went through a transformation of wellbeing. Wellbeing is seen everywhere these days and we even have wellbeing teams we can refer patients to. However, England caught a fever in June of this year and it was World Cup football fever at that. Suddenly the nation was on a tremendous high as the England football team progressed beyond expectations in this four-yearly spectacle. Not only were they a young team to be proud of but their manager played out his role with such poise that we all were full of admiration and I even considered going to work in a waistcoat, his trademark piece of apparel.

But I couldn't help thinking that our government is missing another trick. Not only were surgeries eerily quiet during the World Cup but everyone seemed uplifted with a huge drop in patients presenting with low mood. As important as our 101 wellbeing and mindfulness teams are, maybe a greater impact would be seen by investing even more in encouraging the very best into football from a young age. Then, with more success in international sport for the future there would be the positive effect across the nation. It is said that John Major, the former prime minister, had the idea to invest in Olympic sport at grassroots level and hence we have seen Team GB walk away with loads of medals in recent times, which all rub off well where the nation's mental wellbeing is concerned.

I also see a marked upswing in mood around bank holidays. We are always being told we should have or will be getting more, but it never seems to happen. We seem to be caught up with the idea of days celebrating past sea battle victories and so it falls off the agenda as no one can agree what the day should represent in order to be inclusive. In fact, it need not celebrate anything other than positive time together. Certainly, the four-day break over Easter has a huge effect on people's positiveness for simply being quality time together as family or friends. Perhaps more four-day breaks even four times a year are just what the doctor ordered and would make my life easier as people's wellbeing took a lift.

I am also reminded how mental health services were arranged when I started as an independently practising GP in 1988. Then, we literally had one consultant psychiatrist, a psychotherapist and a community psychiatric nurse covering the whole patch. I am in awe of how they used to manage the workload often with direct dialogue with the GP, even pairing up on home visits to patients in crisis. Now, despite the vast numbers of specialist teams and individuals available, as a GP you still feel like you are firefighting mental health in the practice a lot of the time. Yes, it's great to have all these experts but I cannot help feeling that it's not good value when you think of the resources being spent.

Still, as a GP I am often having to sort out problems despite patients being under mental health services care. Often the patient will have had some very elaborate assessment that no one but a mental health worker could read or understand, as often it doesn't flow like a story and is full of process tick boxes and legal requirements that presumably need filling in order to fulfil some higher assessment by regulators. However, for a busy GP with perhaps 100 letters to read a day it doesn't make easy reading. Then there will be a care plan, often saying there is no mental health need after all, crisis is over now they have been seen and after the cooling off that occurred whilst waiting to be seen, and then if anything is needed it's back to the wellbeing teams for another wait for 'therapy' – either counselling or CBT, cognitive behavioural therapy that is.

Now CBT is all the rage since it was found to be as good as medication for mild to moderate depression, a kind of remapping of thought processes in your brain to make you feel better about yourself and the world. But I would say it's only as good as the therapist you see, ranging from very senior staff and quite inspirational individualised therapy to just starting out personnel, and may be delivered in a group setting. Patients give very differing feedback depending on who delivers it, and of course with the clamber to offer this therapy to as many as possible there aren't enough senior therapists to go round.

Having said that, for some it's a true eye opener to a new way of thinking that changes lives and I would have loved to have had it available when I started out. Back then, having completed posts in psychiatry at senior house officer and registrar level, I would offer a few select patients some basic talking therapy myself. I remember a couple who had unfortunately lost a child, and another who had personality issues that meant them contacting the practice repeatedly, being very much helped by some regular sessional work over a number of weeks at the end of morning surgery. Wow, how I would love to have half an hour for a chance to have a break and a quick wee, let alone spend valuable time helping patients move on in their lives, but those days are gone. Successive governments determined to fill up the GP's day more and more have put paid to that.

Also I miss the regular meeting and discussion with local consultants. Our local psychiatrist is lovely and very approachable. He understands where we are coming from and will relook at a case where we feel the point of the referral has been lost along the way. But somehow our paths do not cross anywhere near as much as before and it never feels that we are working together on patient cases as we once did. With the team approach to psychiatric patient care in community mental health teams (CMHTs) it's easy for patients to be lost in the system and no one takes responsibility.

There is a dilution of responsibility because who ultimately is at the top seeing that the correct diagnosis and treatment is followed? It often falls to the GP to make sure no one falls through the net. Previously, with the consultant model, it was often the case that patients would be looked after at a secondary level for years and so the GP did not need to spend time being involved. There are negatives to this but at least we had more appointments available. It's time this was factored in and GPs had fewer patients to look after per GP to recognise all the extra follow-ups we now do. An absolute must for improving wellbeing of the medical profession as a whole.

CHAPTER 4

JULY/AUGUST

NO GPS AND MY RESIGNATION PROPOSAL

This July/August the lack of GPs has hit the headlines again and it's really hotting up. Apparently we need an extra 6,000 now let alone the 5,000 promised by 2020. It's all looking a bit bleak and I am a bit smug that I have already crossed the average retirement age of 59 with many saying they now plan to go at 55. Against this is a great sadness that it has taken so long to recognise that it's not scaremongering but for real, and health ministers burying their heads and hoping for the best just won't do.

A bit like the global warming we witnessed this summer, we cannot go on ignoring things otherwise we are heading for disaster on a huge scale with our health services, and don't expect the private sector to do any better. So what should be done?

Firstly, we need to fund practices with fewer patients per GP in order to be able to add a GP to a practice without the practice suffering financially. Two thousand heads to a GP is no longer fit for purpose with all the things GPs are expected to do compared to when I started out. With the word that GPs will ultimately have time they need with patients at a pace that is safe to practise this would start to attract doctors back into the practice and maybe help some stay on.

There also needs to be recognition that with the huge rise in nursing homes in a practice area this brings its own issues that destabilise practices and leads to low morale. Practices need proper funding to employ staff to deal with this or homes need to be made to employ a 'matron' to filter sick residents. It is unacceptable that a qualified GP will go out to homes repeatedly to see potentially sick patients because staff cannot do the basics like taking a temperature and it's more than their job's worth to take responsibility themselves.

In our area we are paid to do a fully inclusive ward round at homes once a week to support practices. This is woefully inadequate as homes often request GPs daily or several times a day. In my own practice we have a GP out at least a half day every day to cover the local homes, and it's still not enough and they still keep building them on our patch. Where will it end?

There also needs to be a proper process for allowing practices to expand as their towns expand and not just mop up as in former times when building was slow and population growth more predictable. NHS England needs to have some clout so that there is health planning around town expansion that is properly financed and properly thought out. All I see at the moment is panic and unanswered questions from those who are meant to be sorting the problem, but to give them their due they do not have the resources either, or certainly not enough.

I would also stop the constant drive to open GPs all hours. It makes no sense when GPs and practices are on their knees, and in some areas have closed altogether, that a government makes it one of their vote winners to push practices to open longer. With staff doing 12-hour days as a norm it is inappropriate to expect people to come in for longer hours and weekends without new staff. No wonder retention and attracting new staff has become so difficult. Better to get general practice in good shape and then look to gradual expansion of hours.

If you read the newspapers you would think that there wasn't a GP service out of hours when there is. Admittedly, we would all prefer to see our own GP, but at the moment this is not realistic. Allow general practice to stabilise and thrive, then think of this. Having just seen one of my children become a GP partner after 11 years of training, with all the huge hurdles and number of skills it takes to become a GP these days and pass the difficult exams, including the practical ones mentioned before when trainee GPs have to act out scenarios with actor patients, don't tell me there are thousands of foreign GPs out there trained to this exact level just waiting to come over and save us. It's not an honest conversation or at all realistic. Someone on high better sit up and start planning soon and very quickly.

August also saw three astounding moments for me. Firstly, Dr Bawa-Garba won her case at the Supreme Court. The year started with fear overtaking the medical profession as it appeared that a doctor could lose their career over genuine bad decisions taken in a high pressure moment. Unfortunately, in this line of work like with aeroplane pilots, it can result in devastating consequences. I really feel for the parents of the little boy who died. They must be feeling very upset and bewildered just now.

However, I firmly believe we have judges for a reason. Especially the learned and experienced ones. They are able to sit away from all the emotions generated by such a case and make a considered judgment based on all the facts, and hopefully see it from all sides and understand the implications of decisions for the future. That's what they are good at, in the main. It remains to be seen how this will go forward, but today many doctors and doctors to be will have felt relieved because 'there by the grace'.

Another shocking piece of news was that 400 doctors have committed suicide in the last three years. No way! How did I miss that and why has it not been highlighted before? It's an astonishing and appalling statistic. If ever there was evidence of a broken workforce this is it. I can't really find the words to say how I feel about this and the processes afoot that led to this being so. Shameful. Also the newspapers suddenly woke up to the lack of GPs. This time we are 6,000 short and it will get worse. Despite the fact that it takes about nine years to become a GP, the response from NHS England and thus the government was that they are committed to training more GPs and will look abroad to recruit. Don't get me wrong, the NHS would have long since gone without the help of doctors from Asia, particularly India, and especially so in general practice, but with the bar being placed so high these days for GPs to qualify and pass their exams, remember the CSA, will these doctors have to prove their worth equally? Time will tell.

At the end of the month and with all partners back from their summer holidays we met to discuss retirement dates. As with all negotiations, it didn't quite go as I expected. I had decided not to go exactly on my 60th birthday but maybe shortly after. I also offered to wind down more slowly to allow any new doctor coming in to settle into the role. This went down like a ton of bricks mainly because folk didn't seem able to visualise it, so spring 2019 seems most likely. Both parties have gone away to think.

I also got details on my forthcoming 35-year university reunion. I hurriedly went down the list. What a fantastic turnout it will be but how astonishing that most of my university chums have already retired and that's with me being a year older as I took a year out after the sixth form.

I loved reading what folk were up to. Particularly taken by the guy who says he is now a tattoo model. Seems there is life after retirement after all! There was me thinking more of creative gardening, a new language or tapping into my artistic past and rekindling old skills. Obviously I will need to be more inventive. Maybe retirement will be a sort of rebirth for me after all.

CHAPTER 5

REUNIONS, MAGIC AND CRABSTICKS

And so it was, on an amazingly warm and sunny Sheffield September day, the 29th to be precise, my 35th medical school reunion arrived. For some reason I was very excited indeed. More than I had imagined I would be. Perhaps it was the prospect of finding out what a tattoo model with a medical degree actually looks like. Perhaps it was the fact that I was eager to see what 35 years in the NHS had done to people. Then I worried, what if we had all been changed so much that we couldn't recognise each other.

I have to admit the evening was a strange mix of catching up with friends and colleagues who had not changed one bit, to the rest of the evening which was spent staring at people and wondering if they were spouses; or indeed that rather hip teenager medical student who somewhere along the line went grey, put on three stone and took on a vacant look similar to my own. As the evening progressed most had ditched the name badges so I guess I will never know.

I also had a lot of making up to do as the event happened to coincide with my 34th wedding anniversary. It was leading up to the event that I realised Sheffield is not awash with hotels that would easily make up for such a double booking. Nor would accommodation at the conference centre hired for the reunion dinner do either. As luck would have it I found a nice little boutique hotel overlooking a park just a 10-minute walk from the event.

We celebrated a day early in our room (the best they had) with our dinner served overlooking the park with huge trifold windows folded back. Sheffield put on a great show with more autumnal sunshine blazing through than I think I saw in my whole five years at university. The hotel turned out to be a real gem. Apparently, Picasso stayed there once, which is quite amazing when you think about it. Quite what he found to do in Sheffield is debatable. Perhaps he was short of a set of cutlery. More likely he was there for a peace convention in the 1950s.

I had forgotten just how much I loved Sheffield. Despite misconceptions to the contrary it is one of Britain's greenest cities perched as it is on the edge of the Peak District. It is also one of our largest UK cities but barely gets a mention anywhere, which was a regular gripe and news item when I studied there. On the whole it is much the same except they now have trams when I remember bendy buses instead. They also had the misconceived idea of building a huge shopping centre on an old steel works site out of town which meant a lot of department stores moved out of the centre, which I think a crying shame. However, the centre still has a majestic feel with a revamped peace garden with glorious fountain jets and new winter gardens housed in one of the biggest city centre greenhouses around.

Still the most impressive thing of all is the people. Quite unknowingly they draw you into their daily lives and conversations and it's a work of art. Whether it be discussing shoe sizes in Marks & Spencer's sale as if you are their best friend, a friendly chat whilst queuing for coffee and being involved in a search for a missing wife (I kid you not), all is done in such a charming and natural way that left us feeling a warm and affectionate glow for days afterwards. Why can't we all be like that? Perhaps Sheffield needs to put on courses and raise the nation's mental wellbeing.

Mind you, despite this I do now remember as a medical student I did get a flea in my ear a couple of times. Firstly, daring to ask for cod and chips when "we just 'ave fish up 'ere." Also a friend and I were hurriedly chased out of a bread shop by an old lady brandishing her buns where we had asked, quite reasonably we thought, if they did French bread for a party. We never asked again. You see, you don't insult South Yorkshire folk, but take them as you find them and watch your conversational skills and feeling of wellbeing soar. You will also hear the most down to earth talk and conversations to again warm your heart as you move around.

I will never forget the two old ladies having a whale of a time at the sales chatting away sixty to the dozen, but as one sped through the ladies' department her friend, rather worried that with clothing bargains on their minds they might forget more important things, called out, "Ey luv, don't let me forget m' crab sticks!" Suddenly all was fine, worries dissolved and we left with lovely smiles on our faces all day.

I can't help wondering why I ever left this magical place. I do know actually, it was a shortage of house jobs in Trent Health Authority with a new medical school opening in Leicester and larger intakes all round so that 50 of us did not have the required two house jobs lined up as we faced our final exams. Not to be beaten I applied to the first job I saw in the British Medical Journal and by some miracle I got it. So Luton it was to be rather than Sheffield for my second house job, and I also met my future wife who happens to be a northern lass as well as a fine doctor, so it's not all bad. Thirty-four years of not all bad to be precise.

So I returned south having met up with my mates and slightly more convinced I will retire at 60, as despite being one of the oldest in the year the majority of GPs, consultant surgeons, anaesthetists, pathologists, psychiatrists, you name it, had already retired, exhausted but now reinvigorated. What a waste of talent and how quickly our time as doctors seemed to go by having met up again. After all the studying, 35 years of service seemed to fly past. And what a poor indictment of past governments that such a talented bunch would feel the overwhelming need to hang up their stethoscopes as they became more and more disillusioned. A vast amount of knowledge and expertise had just gone down the drain and mostly I feel unnecessarily so. But then what do I know when comparing to politicians and newspaper editors? I'm just a doctor. Well only for a while it seems.

October saw the return of Lord Darzi. This was a man, quite a nice man as it turns out, but a surgeon, who was given the task of sorting out general practice when Labour was in power. He keeps cropping up as a saviour of all things to do with family medicine and we are all wondering how did he do that? Does he have some kind of hypnotic glance? How can a surgeon know much about general practice let alone save it? Imagine if a GP was to lead the government on futuristic surgery development. It just wouldn't happen and I would like to think that none of my GP colleagues would ever try.

It's like Waitrose running the trains. It wouldn't and shouldn't happen. But somehow it did happen and Lord Darzi invented the GP centres that came to be known as Darzi centres and he got a peerage afterwards. In my area we had such a centre open about eight miles away. Open all hours to attract patients who work and in doing so reduce the bread and butter payments to usual GPs in an area. It's said that our local centre cost £1 million in the first year and during the first few months had about 30 patients. Whether that's exactly true no one knows but it was generally accepted that it was a lot of money for little gain.

Can you imagine if your ordinary and overworked GP had earned £1 million for looking after the equivalent of a classroom of kids. The daily 'rags' would have a field day, but it wasn't generally reported. Governments are obsessed with extending hours without staff, money or data to support the idea and still are. It's not that I would be totally against the idea of these super centres when practices are closed. In fact, Darzi centres duplicated availability by being open all day. Had they had a bit more in the way of resources than your average GP surgery they could have taken a huge burden from A&E.

I often get patients who I have the skills to keep in the community if only I had quick access to blood and X-ray reports and some wait and see time in a safe haven. You see, when the whole world thinks GPs working 13-hour days is not long enough and we should do evenings and weekends in addition as we used to, the X-ray and blood departments close at 4.30pm at the latest so we can never truly deal acutely with patients that need more than just ourselves to heal them. I often have a patient on a Friday that I would love to deal with if only I could get a blood result in two hours as they do in hospital rather than two days.

Imagine this. A Darzi centre, aka a super GP centre with the ability to see such patients and make fast diagnoses. Imagine they were connected like Virgin Airways to a super duper medical consultant for advice. Let's even make the consultant a virtual one, all high tech and available for FaceTiming. They would also be on fast connection to diagnostics. Imagine it was so good virtually all the local GPs wanted to take turns staffing it. It would be awesome. In fact, it wasn't awesome because even though Lord Darzi may be superhuman or akin to Moses, he ain't a GP, so he doesn't know how it works and so these centres fell by the wayside in the main. Expensive duplications of what we already had, but the Darzi GPs didn't know you like your old family doctor, so in that respect worse.

But the good Lord has staying power. This time he came back in the autumn of 2018 with another master plan. He worked out that 70% of what I do could be done by a nurse, and thus as our government looks over the abyss and can see that we will be about 8,000 GPs short in a blink of an eye, he is back in business. Except he is still a retired surgeon and not a GP, and it seems hasn't much of a clue how complex patients are managed in general practice and how important medical training is in sorting out what is what on a day to day basis.

Yes, we have very good nurses and they can do the minor illness stuff with a GP in the wings when it gets complicated or goes off piste, and they can do chronic disease management more dedicatedly than I can with the right protocols and support. But no Lord Darzi, they cannot and do not want to do 70% of what I do because patients present in complex and individual ways that are often not in the books. Also, we the experienced family doctor may be a dying breed, but the family doctor who has known you for 30 years or even 10 years has such unique information about you which makes diagnosis, management and care planning all the more accurate, cost-effective and appropriate. Now you won't get that in any flash walk-in centre where you are an unknown, will you?

So could some nice politician find Lord Darzi a role that he might know something about, really know. That kind of knowing that comes only from those who have worked their system for years and not those in high office who think they know and can convince others that they do. The other worry is that politicians start believing that general practice can be run by anyone other than GPs themselves. We are constantly being told that as GPs we refer too much, then in the next breath not enough. We are constantly told as GPs that we spend too much on drugs but then don't start enough patients on, say, statins. We have directives on cancer and investigations like X-rays for chronic cough which mean many more consultations and more referrals, but there is no account made of this so we get told we aren't offering enough appointments.

Many of these decisions are made by the non GPs. Yet no one realises just how many people I have to run a slight risk with each time I see them otherwise the NHS would come to a huge and grinding halt. It's skill and experience that allows me to do that along with knowing my patients well and reviewing them appropriately.

I know from experience that nurses, emergency care practitioners and physician assistants, whatever you wish to call them or employ to fill the gaps where GPs were traditionally employed, will not want to take risks of this nature so naturally will refer, prescribe, investigate more as is their training. Who could blame them but costs will certainly rise and patients will need to have more done to them. Now this won't always be a bad thing and I think the best GP team is the one with all these people working together.

But just as I would rather Lord Darzi take out my appendix rather than one of my GP colleagues, when it comes to designing future general practice could not I or one of my colleagues with 30-35 years' experience have a say? Let old Lord D go to the Lords and talk his heart out on all things surgical but don't tread on my GP toes, your lordship! You have done it more than enough times.

And so October came to an end and another dose of reunion therapy. This time, my wife's. Her London medical school chose to meet up in the extremely picturesque town of Cheltenham and the lovely autumn of 2018 put on another fabulous display. Luckily for me I have got to know quite a few of her university chums, being either friends or simply because they are very good at meeting up. I also worked in the London area so some became my work colleagues too. Interestingly, although many had retired, a few more from my medical school were still clinging on.

More interesting was the lack of tattooists (or maybe they did it secretly in London), but instead, a collection of magic performing medics at dinner. All presumably self-taught. One actually had a voice like David Nixon who entertained us with his TV magic in the 1960s and 70s. A sort of hypnotic voice. I was mesmerised. Again, I thought how wonderful that doctors can diversify like this. Just like magic. It gave me a sort of warm glow to think that human beings that can be involved in all kinds of healing by day could be so entertaining by night. What is more they were actually very good at it!

From magic to Halloween and thoughts of strange goings on at the practice. Now I may be on the fringes at times and very open minded to most things but generally I have had very little contact with all things supernatural. Despite being involved in many end of life situations, being out all hours alone, particularly in the early years, I have never been abducted by aliens or rarely had any unusual events, but two come to mind.

Our surgery is in a very old building, formerly an old coaching inn. There were stories of the appearance of a rather menacing Roundhead soldier in the building from time to time which would fit in with its history and use. I have never had even a hint of him or anything else for that matter and have always felt safe and relaxed when in the building, including in the early hours collecting equipment to deal with a sick night-time patient. Then one evening something very odd happened. A young man at the counter one dark winter evening screamed out that someone had just given him an enormous kick in the back of his leg yet there was nobody there. He seemed incredulous of the event and kept saying what had happened over and over again even as his girlfriend eased him out of the surgery.

Had our Roundhead struck? Who knows? I still haven't seen him and time is running out.

The most amazing tale of the unexpected for me happened fairly recently. I went to visit an elderly lady in her very historic cottage in the grounds of an old Jacobean mansion. As I walked in she suggested we went to an antechamber. As we passed through her living room I noticed a very smart elderly gentleman dressed like Toad from Toad Hall sitting in the middle of the room. He said nothing. She said nothing as she breezed past. I wished him good morning and he looked right through me with a Mona Lisa look. Later that look would haunt me a little. I thought nothing of it at the time as my patient chatted away as I followed her through.

Our consultation over I went back and the gentleman had gone. Disappeared. The penny didn't drop until a few days later having been reminded and thinking of that strange look. Could he have been a ghost? I never got a chance to ask my patient as she moved away shortly afterwards. However, a couple of years later she was back, this time in a local nursing home. Unfortunately, she had no recollection. Had I seen a ghost? I asked. She didn't know. I suppose I will never know either. He seemed pretty benign and not at all scary. Perhaps I was lucky. I wouldn't know as I've never knowingly seen a spirit before.

No nightmares for me but for some reason a slightly unnerving feeling about the whole event remains with me. It is unexplained and a bit strange. I'll never forget that hypnotic look either.

CHAPTER 6

FLU JABS, APPRAISALS AND ENEMAS

So here I am in November and my resignation letter has gone to my partners and my retirement next year has been accepted. I felt I needed to take the plunge. Things continue to get no better. There is talk of more practices closing. GPs are being blamed for delays in flu vaccination now and the daily rags of the newspaper world have put the knife in again. It seems the truth is that yes, NHS England did announce the need for a new vaccine for over 65s in January, most GPs had ordered by March but the supplier could only get deliveries out in a phased way. Why the need to blame anyone?

What is so bad for GP morale is that the 'we never get anything wrong' NHS England team are telling the press that GPs aren't doing enough. If you can't get your jab don't blame us, blame your GP. GPs are rightly cross and also because two or three years ago we were doing all the flu vaccines perfectly well until some bright spark decided to deregulate the system and let pharmacists and any Tom, Dick or Harry with any idea of how to unsheath a needle give the vaccine instead.

Unfortunately, people or pharmacies do not always let the GP know when it has been given or not given elsewhere so chaos reigns. GPs are meant to target a certain number of at risk patients each year, but now there are so many players it's difficult to know who is left to target and how many vaccines to order. Still they continue to blame us, as we are kind of used to it these days. Sort of inoculated against all these sticks and stones stories, but only so much. You can only vaccinate yourself against so much negativity and fake news for so long.

I haven't announced my departure yet to the patients but they seemed to sense it as this week I had lots of my old characters pitch up I hadn't seen for a while including one who had moved back to the area and was relieved to be back in the fold. He was a youngish guy with seronegative arthritis, all the pain but nothing to show for it, on blood tests that is. He was missing his Co-Proxamol, a paracetamol combination which was banned as it could put little old ladies who look too much into a deep coma or even worse. You see the active other ingredient suppresses breathing if taken in overdosage, which is a very unfortunate way to deal with arthritic joints, especially if you are forgetful.

Equally unfortunate was that it seemed to work well on lots of patients anecdotally but there was no scientific evidence. We now live in a world of evidence-based medicine, EBM (when it suits), so despite many patient protests of it working well with little or no harm, it was removed from the NHS drug tariff. Perhaps there is now evidence of people addicted to Tramadol, codeine and Gabapentin, now commonly used to control orthopaedic pain instead, but you won't hear about that until perhaps it hits the newspapers, then the GPs will be to blame I imagine. Hand me some Co-Proxamol! It might just numb my pain for a while, or will it?

I've become a bit militant this week since I've decided to retire. Such is the crisis developing even in my own Home Counties town, with one practice closed and taken over by us and another having closed its list due to staffing issues, all work now flows to us. We have fired off letters demanding a meeting with NHS England to ask if they will give any support, also I politely asked our MP for a meeting too. Something has to be done otherwise 'this town is heading for a primary care disaster', or that was the general theme.

I have also decided enough is enough with problematic patients. With all lists closed apart from ours we have our fair share of nuisance individuals, and since it has been frowned upon to remove patients, it's causing issues. I do get it that you cannot throw folks off willy-nilly as we used to perhaps, but then we have a lady who has DNA'd, that's short for Did Not Attend, 83 appointments in a year, sometimes having booked an hour or so before, so you have to act.

Then we have a lady who calls us and all emergency services three or four times a day. She is banned from calling an ambulance more than so many times a week, the mental health team won't see her as she has a personality disorder, so it comes down to us. We also now have a man who feels it's perfectly reasonable to keep consulting for an hour at a time and still complains about the service.

So I'm not saying we should remove people all the time and inflict on some poor unsuspecting other GP, but if the powers that be feel it's a good idea to dilute doctors' power then please put something else in place. A kind of NHS police force with a psychologist on board would be good to come alongside these people and say 'enough is enough', 'what's going on here guys?' At least that would be a start and I can plan to do something else with the spare 830 minutes of my time. Stand by NHS England, you are about to get the letter of all letters. I'm not vindictive but with retirement beckoning I'm now feeling unshackled and don't give a damn. Get me my Basildon Bond, I'm on a roll.

It's December and it's ESR time. Now if you said ESR to most doctors they would think instantly of a blood test. An Erythrocyte Sedimentation Rate to be precise. A fairly old test that has stood the test of time. It measures body inflammation and general unwellness. If you put erythrocytes, that's the red blood cells that give your blood its red colour, in a long test tube and allow them to settle, the rate at which they fall indicates the degree of inflammation or serious pathology in your body. So an

ESR of 1 or 2 is generally a good thing although it can be quite normal to be up a bit in older folk.

However, I am talking about Educational Supervisor's Report (ESR). A twice-yearly overview of a trainee GP's progress in their learning. You see, I have been a GP trainer since 1993/4 when I completed what was then a year-long modular course in medical education. After that my practice had to jump through various educational hoops to become a training practice, the biggest task being making sure every set of patient notes, of which we had 10,000 then, had to have a medical summary on the front page should any trainee GP happen to see them.

So nearly 25 years later I have just completed three ESRs for the last time. This involves many hours of work sifting through trainee electronic notes recorded on various patient scenarios or encounters, or other clinical learning called logs, as mentioned before. They add two or three per week over each six months and each has to be tagged with various 'competencies' like being holistic, ethically aware or dealing with complexity and so on. They are expected to cover what is called the GP curriculum so as to have a broad knowledge of family medicine subjects.

On top of this they do WBAs. Work Based Assessments. Basically case discussions and clinical scenarios with a clinical supervisor, generally a consultant or a GP trainer, that are all scored in various skill areas like listening skills, involving patients in their care plan and so on. On top of this they will have to pass a knowledge-based test and you may remember the dreaded CSA (Clinical Skills Assessment) mentioned earlier, taken with actors in London.

So all of this will be collated and assessed every six months with a final write-off at the end of three years. A far cry from when I qualified as a GP when you generally had to complete your said hospital posts, attended half-day release education sessions, and then on completing your year with a GP trainer, get a huge tick and a signature saying you were a good egg. Unless you killed anyone carelessly or wound up your trainer by not doing your job you were home and dry. Clearly this was open to a lot of cosying up between parties and not very fair. Hence the changes which are huge when you think of it.

So I met with my three supervisees and then wrote it all up over a weekend. When else would I do it? I then emailed the East of England deanery and confirmed that was me done. Nearly 25 years of teaching nearing its end and thanks for having me. As well as educator supervising I have had a trainee as their clinical supervisor most years when they do a kind of apprenticeship in your practice for up to a year with you. I have sadly lost count and details of a lot of them. I suppose I never expected to do it for so long.

December also saw me doing my annual appraisal and five-year revalidation. Since the infamous Manchester GP who bumped off a large portion of his patient list we have been required to be appraised every year. I was one of the first to be done. Not because I am infamous or murderous but because as a GP trainer, I and others like me were seen as an easy group for the appraisal system to cut its teeth on. We are meant to know what we are doing. So every year for about the past 10 I have had to present a minimum 50 hours of learning, feedback from colleagues and patients, and other evidence such as audits and significant event analyses to prove to the world that I am still safe to be let loose on patients.

I haven't heard of anyone failing but perhaps I work in an above average area. Every five years all this information is collated and presented to the General Medical Council who, if happy with the evidence, allow you to practise for a further five years. I've decided to stay registered for now in case after formal retirement I decide to keep my hand in and do locums. As it happens, my revalidation has been confirmed just after Christmas, so either the GP shortage is causing anxiety at the GMC or I'm doing OK.

Thinking of Dr Shipman (and I prefer not to dwell on this most evil of doctors) has reminded me of my behaviour at the time the news broke of his misdemeanours. Rumour has it his favourite prime time to inject his patients with a lethal dose of morphine was 3pm. Imagine my panic when asked to visit an elderly lady living alone but with painful cancer who asked me to administer some of her emergency supply of morphine and as I looked at my watch it showed 3pm. What I actually did was to ring her daughter and 'own up' to my proposed actions. She was fine about it and the patient did well. Always better to be safe than sorry I feel.

This month also saw the arrival of my 55-60-year-old personal bowel screen. It was slightly my own fault as I am also the bowel GP lead in the practice. Basically I get all the poo and mini scope results for our patients and then chase up those who decline the test outlining the benefits in a Dear Patient letter. Apparently the personal letter approach is supposed to encourage patients to go through with it. So I rang the Freephone number and asked when I might be getting my bowel screen. Thankfully, before I could say diverticulitis, I had an invitation in the post for a mini scope. They also sent a squidgy sausage that turned out to be an enema. I don't know why I say thankfully but the day happened to be on a day's leave, which I think was brilliant as I wasn't sure how I would give myself an enema in between patients, and keep smiling and retaining for that matter.

As it happens, my dad was also due a transfusion in the same hospital earlier that morning so I had suggested to my wife that I lie down somewhere in the hospital and give the enema to save on a journey to and from my house. She was not impressed and I think was worried I might tarnish my reputation so close to retirement. I was worried I might sully something else. So I had to dash home and for the first time in my 59 years squeeze the contents of a fat unfrozen ice pop into my rectum and hold for five minutes. I actually managed 10 minutes. I'm always up for a challenge. The desired effect and then a dash to the endoscopy suite with dad having blood pumped into him the floor below me.

Feeling very cleansed, I lay on the bed awaiting the endoscopist. It turned out to be the local associate dean who I know well from my GP training and teaching days and who likes to scope people's bowels, when not teaching or being a GP, for a change of scenery. Oh well, who could blame him. There was a high chance I would know the doctor anyway so we decided to proceed and we caught up on medical educational gossip and so forth whilst he manipulated a flexible endoscope around my bowel recesses. It was all good and I felt proud that I had actually done some pretty good bowel prep and all looked very pink and healthy. You don't want to let your endoscopist friends down now, do you?

I also managed to confirm he was still happy to sponsor me for my fellowship application for the Royal College of GPs. Not sure I need to let the college know the circumstances though. Best not mention on the application form. 'How well do you know the applicant?' 'Inside and out' says the sponsor!

As we near the end of 2018 our new health minister takes a break from all the Brexit woes to make three announcements and I ain't happy. It's not that I don't like him. In fact, he hasn't got the scary stare of the last one and on the whole has what my gran would have called a kind face, but I can't help thinking he is a bit out of his depth and naive. It seems the NHS and all who sail her will at first be saved by several amazing pieces of health policy he plans to lead on.

The first is that we are all to be on a new super duper computer network so all GPs, hospitals and health workers can interact and see the same patient records. Apparently this is going to free up hours of my time. Now I don't know about you but did computerisation ever free up the time we were promised? Answer that after you have just signed off your hundredth email of the day! It also sounds very grand, ideal and very expensive. Didn't the chief executive of Cambridge's showcase university hospital, said to have been the best CEO there had ever been, have to resign when the new computerisation project blew the budget so much the A&E was threatened with closure, which in business terms was bankruptcy of the hospital?

And why oh why have all the practices in one half of my own county just gone over to a new computer system called Systm1 (that's right no 'e') which is the same for everyone so that GPs, emergency services, community services and A&E can share information in the interest of patients, when we all had perfectly good systems before, albeit isolated ones, if it's going to be all change again? Is this good use of resources when we are dealing with austerity and can't even feed our nation adequately or go to a library anymore, let alone drive on a pothole-free road? Does the health secretary actually know that many areas have already upgraded at considerable cost? Maybe he knows HS2 will ultimately be cancelled.

I was further angered by the notion that practices will have less work as a result. Apart from my administration staff not having to scan on letters from hospitals to patient records as they will automatically 'come down', I cannot see that will save GP time, and in fact may erode it. You see already we are finding on our new system that other services send messages to the patient's GP. Oh, no they don't! Well it is pantomime season. Sorry they do. In fact, the system will select the patient's registered GP rather than the GP they usually see. People don't really understand this, including it seems half of the people who work in the NHS outside general practice and possibly the health minister.

So whereas now my staff will direct letters to the appropriate doctor, if in the future they arrive in my inbox by mistake that's another chore for me redirecting to a colleague. Imagine this and it's hard to grasp. We look after an intermediate care unit. I told you before. In the old days we called it a convalescence unit or rehabilitation unit. As it's full of frail elderly people deemed fit for discharge but not home (Oh no they're not! Sorry again but that's another story) we have a huge drug budget overspend not of our making.

The local health group (CCG) could not separate our budgets but invented a fictitious doctor to keep track of the two budgets. That is our drug budget for our usual patients and the one for the rehabilitation patients under a make believe doctor, and only temporarily under our care and over which we have little authority to change medication easily to cheaper versions. Imagine our surprise when Trusts, that's hospitals to you and me, started sending out discharge letters to this fictitious doctor! You kind of give up at that point.

The other 'good news' was that GPs will be Skyping all their patients and will have so much free time they will feel like they are on one endless holiday. Now, we already do telephone consultations at my practice and do you think we can get people off the phone under 10 minutes, which is still quite ridiculously the average face to face time you get with your GP? Hasn't changed in years. So I can't see where the saving is. Often you can't do half the things you want to do without the patient beside you, and your medical defence company who insures you hates it too and is very liable to up your premiums as a result, so where's the gain? I am sorry but I think it's nothing more than a piece of theatre or even a pantomime.

The other ugly sister seems to be Mr Hancock's announcement that he will create the best maternity services ever. Recent statistics have been very embarrassing for our NHS. Our local Trusts seemed to have escaped the newspapers compared to areas like Shropshire, but I for one haven't seen so many stillbirths as we now see or hear about for decades. So what's going on? Certainly, there is a grave shortage of midwives and women are left far too long without supervision. In recent years after a landmark study saying it was OK, it's been trendy to let women carry on pregnant up to 43 weeks, that is three weeks after usual delivery.

Very cruelly I feel, one of our patients who had a stillbirth at 39 weeks and pregnant again was going to be induced at 39 weeks. I think in that situation some flexibility and understanding was called for, so what's wrong with 38 weeks? If it was me I would have lain on the floor and threatened to pull it out myself.

So, better maternity services are a good thing, yes? Of course they are, but what gets me is we have been letting the service die for years and years so why allow this to happen in the first place? The NHS and Her Majesty's ministers are good at this. They underinvest for years and services crumble until a new incumbent needing to show his worth wants to build it up again. How utterly ridiculous and a cause of unnecessary misery. There can be nothing worse than a bad outcome to one's pregnancy when, with the right investment and midwives with time to care, it could be so different. So I'm all for the health secretary's Christmas good news, but if the service had been supported in the first place would it be necessary? Good luck to him for wanting to create 'the best maternity services in the world' but he had better have his Aladdin's lamp ready.

CHAPTER 7

I'M SIXTY, SUICIDAL PHARMACISTS AND A SUFFOLK SUNRISE

It's a new year and retirement seems very close. The government has taken time out from Brexit to launch a 10-year plan. Unfortunately, they now admit they can't reach their projected GP numbers for 2020 and I feel a bit guilty leaving soon, however workload continues to climb. Due to local practices closing or in emergency measures we are taking all new patients, up 400 in four months. It isn't that I don't want to work, but at just shy of 60 I have run out of energy.

We had an emergency meeting with NHS England over local patient list closures which is severely impacting on us. A master stroke was to invite our patient group who ate them alive. It occurred to me why are these decisions made behind closed doors with a formula which clearly disadvantages practices that can provide a service? Better for all local practices to get round a table with their patient representatives and thrash out a rescue plan. Needless to say, I can't see one meeting changing the situation.

Apparently I'm also leaving because of the pension pot cap. You see, once you leave your student and junior doctor days behind you, you quickly build up a substantial pension pot over 35 years with long hours and a good salary, although this has gone backwards over the last 10 years. Always on the lookout for savings, the government decided to put a cap on the total savings and tax any savings over. If I'm honest the only thing it probably decided was who left first, me or my doctor wife, but it seems a lot of GPs are retiring at 55 when the pot is full. It seems this has rattled new health secretary Matt Hancock's cage.

January is proving stressful as dad is ill again. I rang about an emergency appointment arranged by the hospital but ironically hospital internal referrals are not subject to the two-week to be seen policy as for GPs. So if you have suspected cancer, best not have another hospital department diagnose it. What utter nonsense. So his GP will start the process again and have to do the work instead, wasting more time.

This week the lack of common medicines drove me crazy and hits the news. As duty doctor I spent at least half an hour of precious time reissuing alternatives to often-used drugs. As I pondered on why and how, this story hit the news later in the week. We are told that there are easily found alternatives. Not quite so. Some chemists don't like to commit to suggesting an alternative so then you can waste more time issuing one prescription after another only to be told they are all unavailable. Look at Naproxen. This is a popular anti-inflammatory we are encouraged to use but in short supply. It's the only anti-inflammatory that is deemed safe in people with or at risk of heart disease, so what should the GP do? Say you give an alternative, who would be to blame if a patient was harmed? And who will warn each patient over the switch? The GP, pharmacist or pharmacy counter staff? It's not easy in a busy clinic when patients are champing at the bit and have been primed to think it's easy to switch.

Then there are those drugs that are massively expensive in other doses. That will put a huge hole in the GP drug budget. Who will highlight to a patient that they need to halve or double a tablet as its strength has changed? It's a minefield. No, this new development is worrying in many aspects, and as doctors are encouraged to use more and more drugs according to protocol, the range of options and pressure on supplies will not be easy to solve.

Also this week, another target was announced. Antibiotics to be reduced by a further 15%. Now this seems a sensible approach but what really gets me is it's always GP focused. The headlines always refer to GPs risking our futures by overuse. Certainly this was true and great strides have been taken to reduce use and educate patients. But what gets me and sticks in my throat more than a case of tonsillitis is how hospitals, particularly A&E, use antibiotics, including so-called blacklisted ones, with impunity.

Take the antibiotic Co-Amoxyclav. Once used widely in general practice it's now one that is held in reserve, except for A&E it seems. If you are a little old lady who gets trundled into casualty and 'off legs' as geriatricians might say, in all likelihood you will have your wee dipped with one of those magic urine sticks, and when it turns all the colours of the rainbow, which it surely will, the casualty officer will declare you have a urinary tract infection, or UTI in the trade, and give you antibiotics, and quite likely it's Co-Amoxyclav too and yet there will be no sanctions against the ever so clever hospital.

If I give Co-Amoxyclav and the patient suffers harm like a chronic and potentially lethal bowel infection, I will have a seven-page document to complete and several sleepless nights. Also, in my area, particularly in nursing homes, we no longer wee dip. In fact, we have had a do not dip campaign. The thing is, in elderly ladies in particular, they often have stuff in their wee so you can expect the dip sticks to turn all sorts of colours depending on the time of day, so it's basically worthless.

So GPs now will only treat acutely if there are definite symptoms and the patient is ill, otherwise we await the so called MSU (midstream urine) conducted under laboratory conditions. Unfortunately, it takes three days to process so you can see why a casualty department has a vested interest in diagnosing as many old ladies with UTIs as they can and shift them home, but why should it be so different? These mixed messages drive me crazy and must be very confusing for the patients. Why oh why can the chief medical officer not get to grips with this and be as hard on hospitals as GPs?

I am very much for this reduction in antibiotics but I would like some honesty from the top. Recently there has been a huge increase in scarlet fever cases coinciding with the move away from antibiotics. Scarlet fever arises after a bacterial infection of the throat with an organism called Streptococcus, but Public Health England say they cannot explain this rise in cases. Really? Doesn't take a lot of working out. Obviously we need better ways of detecting sore throats that need antibiotics and it seems the ever so inventive Danes have done this.

Family doctors in Denmark have so-called CRP machines on their desks for when an 'is it bacterial or not?' question needs answering as a matter of urgency. CRP or C-Reactive Protein is markedly raised in bacterial infection. So the clever Danes have found a way to detect bacteria that need antibiotics from viruses that do not. I would imagine patients and parents are far more persuaded to soldier on without treatment knowing their CRP level is normal. It would be great to have the same here but perhaps the funds are to be directed to GP online consultations instead.

This week saw me being equally wound up by secondary care and I was left wondering if CEOs of hospitals ever sit in their own hospital departments and observe what goes on. Dad is back in hospital and this time under haematology. It took a visit to the local cancer centre to try to make a diagnosis of why he has become so anaemic. That wasn't so bad, except some people had waited three hours to be seen. How can that be right?

Luckily, as it turned out our consultant was a faster worker but then we needed blood tests. This involved going to another department and joining another queue, which some people told me can be another two hours. Fortunately for us it was only half an hour. I assume some of those people were already on chemotherapy so why would you expect a fragile, tired, immunologically vulnerable and scared person to queue for up to two hours with all the coughs and colds around them? Could not a blood nurse, phlebotomist, be positioned in the cancer centre?

Then we were sent to the hospital pharmacy. Now if there was a place representing hell on earth this was it. A very cramped department, not at all wheelchair friendly, with hordes of grimacing patients and staff who looked ready to slit their throats. When we arrived we queued to be given a ticket that had a number on it and an estimated waiting time. It said two and a half hours. The fact that these medicines could be easily obtained in the community was irrelevant as hospitals use different types of prescription pads. I already know this of course but what is the sense of that?

Having sat down we noticed a kind of Argos who's next computer board tracking the various numbers which was very hard to read and the only help it gave was to inform you that the numbers had been allocated randomly. No good 172 getting excited when 171 was called. No one dared jump the queue when the board indicated the medicines might be ready as we had all been there long enough to work out that the harassed pharmacist would call out your name at the moment you should move forward. We had already witnessed two fights when someone frantic for overstaying the car park or because his sick wife was about to faint had tried to queue jump.

So we quietly sat at the back and used the time to concentrate on deep breathing exercises. I then heard one of the counter staff say the average wait was an hour so I put my glasses back on to check our ticket which clearly said two and a half hours. So we waited with no idea of what would happen. All of this occurred under a private-looking logo suggesting this hospital pharmacy may be out to tender, which if true I hadn't realised before. Being out to tender in the NHS often means running a service for peanuts, so don't expect any slick service here, nor any department awash with pharmacists. I think the logo also said 'working for you'. It said nothing about speed of working. In the end we waited about 45 minutes so I suppose we should be grateful, if not a little confused over the messages given.

Now GPs may be the scapegoats for the whole NHS, especially in the tabloid press, but we are a pretty entrepreneurial bunch. We have been using computers for consultation note taking and prescribing for years, and for several years now have sent prescription requests via an electronic computer system to any pharmacist we care to. Of course they are mainly local ones but I believe I could send a prescription to the Outer Hebrides if I so wished. That's assuming they have a pharmacist there who is also on the NHS spine as it's called.

So I am left wondering why in this day and age in our hospitals they still write prescriptions by hand and patients trot off clasping it to the pharmacist who doesn't know they are coming. Why not have a computer system that starts the ball rolling by creating an electronic prescription in the outpatients. Then as you wind your way to the pharmacist and navigate the many hospital corridors, the tablets will already be being counted out. Better still, allow some local chemists to be on the list. If they are specialist drugs, have a select group of local pharmacists that stock these and save the agonising expressions on the faces of the pharmacists and patients in my local hospital.

You could even use some of Matt Hancock's special fund for GP Skype consultations before he destroys the patient-family doctor relationship completely. There, sorted. Please don't let me sit in that department again anytime soon and if you see a man in a grey suit in the pharmacy with a notepad making notes let me know. Perhaps it will indicate a new revolution in hospital management techniques.

All of this got me thinking. If this is the best we can do then shouldn't we go back to the drawing board?

I can't quite believe it but a whole year has gone past and I have now reached 60. Sounds awful when you think of it; 59 sounded so much younger. I start to fret that people born in the 1950s are already being admitted to the local nursing homes. It's scary. There is no guarantee of quality of care in homes these days either.

This year I made sure I was first in the queue for the holiday board, so we spent a nice few days on the snowy Suffolk coast. Such was my relief we even got up on my birthday to watch an east coast sunrise and it was worth it. I have to admit watching the sun come up often leaves a lump in the throat much more so than a setting sun. Somehow you realise so much more the majesty of two heavenly bodies of Sun and Earth pivoting around each other as they have done for billions of years.

Have I retired? Well not quite. After much deliberation and discussion, the accountant won through so I'm going at the end of the financial year in March. Ironically that's the planned Brexit day so just about every news bulletin reminds me of the number of days to go. I decided last week to count the actual number of working days. Allowing for holiday, weekends, time in lieu and days off, I calculated I had another 23 days to work. That shocked me a bit. It's shocked the patients too. Suddenly it's dawned on people I have looked after for over 30 years that their most recent visit to see me is likely to be their last. It felt awkward but nice at the same time.

Good and bad together however is never fully satisfactory. Certainly people have said such lovely things, truly wonderful things, but then how do you say goodbye in the dying seconds of a consultation when you have supported, sometimes cried with and seen people through all sorts of crises? Seen them grow old and their children grow up, remembering perhaps when they were first thinking of children. It all feels a bit flat. Too sudden. Unprepared. An anticlimax. A bit like Boxing Day.

I hadn't really thought this through. I don't suppose the patients have, but I have never severed links with so many people at once that for many will have been such close relationships, sharing the most intimate of information and experience. I haven't done this before so it was hard to prepare. I suppose it will be easier when every patient is linked up to a computerised doctor instead. It will be easier to switch off once they get to the end of their useful working life and start all over again with an even more sophisticated model. Talking of which, Matt Hancock was in the news again focusing on his vision for the NHS and I feel my blood pressure going up again. Maybe my imminent retirement will save me taking blood pressure medication, assuming we can still access medicines.

How can someone in the job five minutes have a vision? A vision that seems to totally disregard or value the traditional GP to patient relationship. He's on about his IT revolution again. And ever heard of asking people experienced in their roles as to what would be their vision? What would be their priorities to rescue the NHS without wasting money we can ill afford? No such luck.

It seems that the number of GPs continues to fall this week too, and advertisements and incentives are being made to Australian doctors. Uproot, come and work in the not so sunny UK where house prices are through the roof, Brexit has potentially left the country facing a massive crisis and we will give you a £15,000 bonus. I really cannot see this attracting the number of Aussie doctors we would need. Why not ask UK GPs in their 50s and 60s what would make them stay on? I can tell you it isn't the money they are after. Why not ask them Mr Hancock, are you there? We could link up via Skype if you prefer.

Just when Mr Hancock was starting to irritate more and more he went for an Oscar this week. Suddenly, GPs being criticised again, no surprise there then, but this time over postage. Letters, envelopes and stamps to be precise. Apparently we need to use email more. Is that so? Does he not know just how much we already email, including receiving hospital letters and sending referrals? What really got to me was singling out GPs and not knowing his job. The basis of his rant was that we could save the NHS shedloads of money if we simply emailed.

Unfortunately, the poor unfortunate new secretary of state for health, who looks more and more startled every time he appears on TV, hasn't realised the most important thing about GPs. That is we are independent contractors. That means we buy our stationery and pay for our own stamps. We lick them ourselves with no expense to the NHS at all. This makes his position very dodgy to me but the newspapers still pick up on it and wave their big 'naughty GPs' stick in their headlines. Again.

If we can leave GPs alone for five minutes, I think there is a lot to be saved from local Trusts (that's hospitals to you and me). Ditching postage where possible would produce a huge saving. I remember sitting in my local ENT department waiting for ear suction. A consultant friend suggested I sit and wait when I went deaf one day and it was a great opportunity to observe. Nearly every patient came out needing a follow-up appointment in three to six months. The two very smiley and sweet receptionists (why two?) told everyone they would send out appointments in the post and wouldn't be consulting people's diaries. Actually, they didn't say the last bit but it occurred to me it's bloody relevant. As I was last in I heard them say at the end of the clinic to their supervisor how they were off to post the appointments! Really! Anyone who has an elderly relative under a hospital will know that they get about five letters per appointment, with so many cancellations and re-bookings.

So Matt do your homework, leave the GPs to their personally funded franking machines and make sure you get the hospital outpatient procedures licked, but not the stamps!

I've also had an idea. It's brilliant. Matt would love it. Instead of tying your GP up for 10 minutes on a Skype call rather than seeing him or her face to face, why not have consultants do telephone, email or Skype calls for hospital outpatient follow-ups instead? No need for huge overrunning clinics with endless numbers of nurses and receptionists running around the specialists at great expense. The roads would be empty and the hospital car parks too. What utter bliss. Makes sense to me anyway.

It reminds me of another time I sat with a relative in outpatients. There seemed more nursing sisters, nurses, healthcare assistants and receptionists than patients. Suddenly a loud shriek went around the department. Consultant Mr X didn't have couch paper rolled out on the patient examination bed! My goodness what a failure! Would this affect their CQC rating? This seems an anachronism to me. I have to admit I didn't do the how to extend a paper roll on the couch training course. I sort of worked it out. It's just a big loo roll that naturally unrolls. You hold one end and roll the other. When finished you throw it away and start again. Surely, a man or woman who can hook a kidney stone out of a patient blindfolded in minutes can handle that. But obviously some don't and the NHS pays someone to do it. Bit pathetic really but you won't find that in the national rag. Unless of course it's a GP. Luckily when it comes to paperless GP practice, the only paper in sight is on the couch beautifully placed by yours truly.

Just when I was thinking of how I hate all health secretaries and looked back nostalgically at all the real howlers we have had this past 35 years, Matt says something nice.

Apparently he has read Dr Adam Kay's book and had a road to Damascus moment. He seems to be genuinely apologetic for his predecessor's management of the junior doctors. He is very sorry. Maybe worried-looking man has a heart unlike his stony-faced colleague who vacated the post. They need to be sorry because what happened was in nobody's interest and has led to a drop in the popularity in medicine just when we need more doctors.

The renegotiated weekend rosters were particularly harsh for women doctors with children working in difficult fields like surgery and paediatrics, and for some made it impossible to carry on. In fact, we learned that junior doctors aren't actually necessarily junior either. A registrar or senior registrar is basically a consultant in waiting with years of experience, so was it fair to change their contracts based on some dodgy and convenient weekend death statistics with our Jeremy digging his heels in and deciding instead to work our hospital doctors to death? As we know, some did take their lives but don't expect anyone to own up to that one. Perhaps Matt will be different. Perhaps the whiff of a new independent grouping and nicer face of politics is a natural result of what's gone before. I very much hope so.

Postscript: *Having had lots of time for blue-sky thinking in the hospital pharmacy, I dared to ask if I could collect my dad's drugs* *the following day at a more local hospital — they said yes! I'm so happy I could hug a pharmacist. What was two hours of waiting is a 20-minute drive instead without a wait and dad's risk of a pressure sore in his wheelchair is drastically diminished. It's so good but I'm a bit bemused that I had to have the idea.*

CHAPTER 8

TIME TO GO, TEARS AND A STAG CALLED STEVE

I'm starting to get nervous about leaving and having had weeks of praise and presents I've just had a week of weeping patients not wanting me to leave, and boy was it exhausting. I overran big time and there were many awkward moments. Being a retirement 'virgin' I had no more idea than they did on how to end the consultation for the last time. We kind of got round it by saying our trolleys would very likely bump into each other in Tesco and as I'm staying on the medical register I'll probably be back before they even noticed I had gone. I dare not say that was very unlikely to happen as I had seriously run out of tissues. It left me drained and guilt ridden.

I also decided to email local consultants via a trusted GP liaison officer to say I was going. I got lovely emails back and some of the things said got me thinking of the 'good old days' when we had time for a weekly lunch with the consultants and how valuable this was for networking and saving on patient referrals. Sadly, as we got busier, hospital car parks filled up and got expensive, this tried and tested system bit the dust.

Last week at our local TARGET meeting, which stands for Time for, Audit, Research, Governance, Education and Training, a local gastroenterologist bemoaned the passing of lunchtime education and how he doesn't know the local GPs anymore. You see, someone loves us or at least misses us. TARGET is a funny old thing as it involves every practice closing for an afternoon every three to four months in our area with 111 taking the calls. It does allow some education but mainly it's for our CCG to get new policies out to us and seems an awfully expensive way to do it, plus the fact you spend all week on catch up due to the lost appointments. I somehow feel the weekly lunchtime thing worked better, and apart from the cost of the vegetable lasagne was as cheap as chips and highly effective. It built relationships between medical colleagues which now no longer happens.

So here I am with two weeks to go. My leave date is the proposed (at the moment) Brexit day minus a few lieu days. I will be 60 and two months exactly. Mrs May continues to struggle with the Brexit date and I find myself saying I preferred Mrs Thatcher. Just shows how irritating the PM has become. Mrs T is back in the news this week with personal papers released. At least you knew where you were with her, which is really saying something having been a junior house officer on call in Rotherham, as previously mentioned, on the day of the bloodiest riot and police charge at Orgreave colliery in 1984 during the miners' strike. Absolute carnage. Disgraceful period in our political history. How we didn't lose a few miners that day to their crush injuries on my ward, I do not know. I guess we were all lucky. Anyway, best leave it there. I can feel my blood pressure going up again.

I have started having a spring clean and have enjoyed telling the staff I have been 'tidying up my drawers' which has produced the desired little titter each and every time to lighten my and their mood I suppose. I'm amazed at the things I have kept over the years but I'm managing to be ruthless (Jeremy Hunt would be proud) as I can see no use now for my diabetic demo pens, teaching manuals, plans of the proposed new surgery, eight years behind schedule at the moment, and my set of De Bono hats. How I loved my De Bono hats. A very useful tool for trainee teaching sessions and practice meetings. It's a bit like Harry Potter's sorting hat but used for solving problems not school house allocations. I could tell you about them some time or you could just go to Google. After all, IT is the future. Ask Matt. I wonder which hat he would go for?

So, it's my last week and it feels very strange. Not quite the condemned man perhaps but a slight feeling of foreboding. After all, as I said, I haven't retired before. Patients are still coming to say their final goodbyes. Some if not all are saying the loveliest things and giving very generously from free rail tickets to £50 garden vouchers. Apparently they have had a collection too and it's apparently big. I'm not allowed to know how much.

One lady reminded me of how I supported her when she lost her baby shortly after I arrived as a doctor here and we both said goodbye with a tear in our eyes. No one said it was going to be this hard. I remember thinking I wouldn't have been able to do that Matt, wired up to a computer screen. Thank goodness for old-fashioned general practice and face to face consulting. She had appreciated it for all those years.

This week saw me do my last on call day, which if I'm honest is probably the thing I find hardest now I have slowed up with age. It's a constant barrage of calls and tasks and patients to be fitted in after all the routine stuff is full, which of course it is every day these days. Gone are the afternoons of yesteryear when we finished at 5.20 and had a two-hour lunch break on Fridays to catch up on the week. Lucky to get a toilet break these days.

I had expected to be happier on my last on call day. I worked out that I had done about 1,800 on call days as a GP allowing also for weekends and out of hours sessions in the past. As it turned out, it was quite frustrating as having had a reasonable workload during the day for a change, I had a flood of calls at 5.45 just as my partners were finishing their evening surgeries, so I would have to deal with them all by speaking on the phone, arranging for them to come in to see me before my reception staff start reaching for their coats and the local chemists start shutting up at 6.30. I found myself getting irritated at how so many people were leaving it until the last minute tonight which was something I wasn't going to let happen. Not on my last session. I wanted to go out on a high, not grumpy. Perhaps it is time to go.

I arrived home to another email from a consultant colleague. This time, a bit different. Yes, he still mentioned how they and my patients would miss me but this time they invited me for some pickle ball!

Now, you can take the boy out of the East End but you can't take the East End out of the boy. My mother was originally from Hackney and so on one of the foggiest days in 1950s London I decided to arrive three weeks early whilst she visited her mother, my granny, and thus I was born with the East End label attached. Apparently it was touch and go as the ambulance slowly made its way through the biggest pea soup smog in years with a man with a flare walking in front of the ambulance. Quite a spectacle don't you think?

Anyway, as a consequence I love pickles. I think most East Enders do, after pie and mash that is. Gherkins, walnuts, onions, Piccalilli, you name it, I can't get enough of the stuff; but I had never heard of a pickle ball. Turns out it's nothing to do with condiments at all but a cross between badminton, tennis and table tennis for the over 60s. Trust a retired paediatrician to be kid enough to give it a go and apparently there is a local venue for it. So here I am again, wondering what on earth my future holds, but at least I will have my pickle ball to look forward to.

It's here and I don't know what to make of it. My final day. This week has ended as I started my story with dad in hospital again, so I didn't get much time to reflect. My last day sort of popped up unexpectedly. Of course I knew it was my last day but I couldn't quite believe or feel it. Unfortunately, it was my turn to be on the 7.30am start. No favouritism for the old boy leaving there then. So I rushed through my day wondering what it would feel like as I finally signed off. I needed to finish on time as my colleagues and staff were taking me out for a drink. The posh leaving meal is in a few weeks.

I got there and like when I started in 1983 and passed my final exams it was a bit of an anticlimax. I had always remembered my first patient but wondered what would be my final act as a doctor. Well, as it happens, it was a last minute booking for a patient with anal symptoms. One for the photo album? I think not. Good perhaps that I was brought down to earth at the end. Good perhaps not to feel too self-righteous. And so it was, I logged off for the anal time – I mean final time. No more sad stories to listen to. No more problems to solve. No more top down regulations from the department.

A quick dash to a local pub with a room and a reminder of one of the reasons work can be good for you if you build a good team of people around you. People who turn out day after day with little time to be sick themselves for another daily round of working hectically, which is general practice these days. I love them all and by all accounts they love me back. The money they raised bought a huge bronze stag (or hart) for my beloved garden and very apt for a Hertfordshire boy. They decided to call him Steve. For some reason my staff felt he should have a name.

The day after it happened. I'm back in the surgery with wife support and clearing my room of the last 31 plus years. Luckily I'm pretty tidy anyway and I had been doing the odd bit of sorting over the months but I was amazed what I had kept, including file upon file of assessments of former GP registrars before it all went on line. In each I had left their leaving card. Another episode of a doctor moving on and I felt blessed to have been part of making the doctors of the future. GP training had been a large and rewarding part of my career. I always said if I hadn't been a doctor I would have been a teacher or a forester. But that's a long story. My own school assessments had thrown up some interesting career options for me.

Then it was time to go. My room looked amazing. I found a dermatology atlas (that means a book with pages and pages of skin rashes to aid diagnosis) that my predecessor had left with his name in, so having added mine in 1988 I added my replacement's name for her first day and left it open on the bookshelf. I turned to leave. "Goodbye room," I said. Bad move. Suddenly I remembered all the tears that had been shed and mopped up in that room and I began to cry. No sobbing or anything like that. As a semi-orphaned child I had learned very early on to hold back the tears.

I then realised how honoured I had been to be that person for so many people over all those years. I knew deep down I no longer had the energy to carry on being that person, but the emotion of that transition caught me unawares as the lock clicked on my consultation room door for the final time. This doctor can't see you now I thought. I just hope the new batch of doctors coming next will be given the time and space to do what I did, day in and day out, for half the lifetime of our remarkable NHS.

EPILOGUE

A letter to Matt Hancock, Secretary of State for Health and Social Care, or whoever it might be should your tenancy be short.

Dear Matt

I know you haven't been in the job long but you need to move quickly. You have been put in charge of one of the most precious things we have, called the NHS. Within it work an amazing group of people, but they are on their knees with the workload and have been for years, which isn't safe or fair. Many good people have left. Some have taken their lives. Unfortunately, your predecessor took them for granted and when they were at their most vulnerable changed their working practices and extended their hours. This was bad and I think you realise that now.

I think with austerity we could all see it might be sensible to tighten our belts as a nation for a while to deal with the country's debts but it has gone on too long. Again it has affected the vulnerable the most, caused immense hardship and increased pressure on the health services as social care disintegrated. I never thought I would see a time in the relatively affluent area in which I work, when seeing a depressed businessman who had fallen on hard times, hungry and struggling to make ends meet, that I as a doctor had nothing to offer but the £10 in my pocket. Shame on you and your colleagues for allowing this and not having to feel the pain yourselves.

I have just retired as a GP of 31 years and I beg you to stop the drive towards computerisation of the GP consultation. Dealing with people and their health worries is not just about a tick box exercise on a computer screen. Nor is being a doctor just about diagnosis, however important. It's about being with people on life's journey and in each other's presence as they grapple with their health and their worries. That's the amazing thing about being a family doctor.

So what are you going to do? Will you start listening to those of us who have been in the NHS 30 times longer than you? Are you going to value what we have had for 70 years including the people who work for you on the frontline and make the NHS what it is? You need to Matt, and do it soon. You haven't got long.

I would suggest as a recent GP you make a loud statement that you plan not just to recruit more and more GPs, which you can't honestly achieve in the present situation, but you give hope for future doctors contemplating general practice that things will get better. A commitment to improved resources for practices and a move to reduce the official number of patients per GP within the shortest timescale possible. Two thousand patients per GP is excessive with an increasingly complex population with greater expectations they will be dealt with in primary care. A commitment to support practices with large nursing homes, often several, within their area. A commitment to support practices to employ more staff like frontline physiotherapists of which there are plenty out there. A commitment to stop trying to score election points by spending money you haven't got on misguided schemes like GP extended access and draining staff of any stamina they once had.

But most of all to listen and understand. The craft of general practice has always been about human relationships and a relationship between a person and their doctor and how their health affects them, their family and their position in it. In fact, this is still the bedrock of what we teach our trainees even today and there are hundreds of teaching models, books and publications on the subject. Do you plan to rewrite all of this? Do you realise how much money GPs and their staff save you by knowing their patients really well? So enough of this online consulting stuff. Yes, it will have a place, but do not make it your mantra at a crucial time like this. Act now Mr Hancock before it's too late.

Often you realise how precious something is once you no longer have it. In that you and I might just be the same.

Yours truly,

Dr David Maddams

NHS Doctor 4.7.1983-31.3.2019
Family Doctor 1.1.1988-31.3.2019

ABOUT THE AUTHOR

David Maddams lives in Hertfordshire with his GP wife. Both children studied medicine suggesting they never listened to a single word their parents said.

He has been medical editor to the magazine *4 Girlz* and was recommended for Fellowship of the Royal College of GPs in September 2019.